BRADMAN & PACKER

The deal that changed cricket

DANIEL BRETTIG

www.slatterymedia.com

The Slattery Media Group Pty Ltd

Level 39/385 Bourke Street, Melbourne

Victoria, Australia, 3000

Text © Daniel Brettig, 2019

Design © The Slattery Media Group Pty Ltd, 2019

Published by The Slattery Media Group, 2019

A catalogue record for this
book is available from the
National Library of Australia

Group Publisher: Geoff Slattery

Editor: Russell Jackson

General and project manager: Jeffrey Sickert

Art Direction, Cover Design and Typeset: Kate Slattery

Printed in Australia by Griffin Press

slatterymedia.com

BRADMAN & PACKER

The deal that changed cricket

2 SPORTS SHORTS

**ESSAYS ABOUT REMARKABLE SPORTSPEOPLE
& MEMORABLE EVENTS**

Bradman & Packer is the second of Slattery Media Group's *Sports Shorts* collection, a new home for lively and engaging writing on sport. Every instalment will illuminate or entertain, all the while fitting into your back pocket on the way to the game.

ABOUT THE AUTHOR

Daniel Brettig is the author of the award-winning *Whitewash to Whitewash* (Penguin), which won the Australian Cricket Society's Jack Pollard Trophy for the best Australian cricket book published in 2015. Brettig had been a journalist for eight years, first with *The Advertiser* and then *AAP* in Adelaide and Sydney, when he joined *ESPNcricinfo* in March 2011. There he remains the Australian correspondent. Among other publications, he has written for *Wisden Australia*, *Wisden*, *Inside Edge*, *The Cricketer* and *Sports Illustrated India*.

Contents

AUTHOR'S NOTE

It can be a challenging task to write about events for which many of the principal characters are no longer around—not least Sir Donald Bradman and Kerry Packer. The following interviewees were extremely helpful, and where quoted have been done so with a present tense "says" or similar: Ian Chappell, Greg Chappell, Mark Taylor, Malcolm Gray, Bob Merriman, David Richards, Lynton Taylor, Jim Fitzmaurice, Brian Mossop, Alan Shiell and James Sutherland. Other sources included Australian Cricket Board minutes and assorted correspondence from private collections, plus the list of books, newspapers and websites cited at the conclusion of this volume.

Daniel Brettig,
January 2019

Preface

One Saturday morning in early 1996, Ray Martin's home phone rang. On the other end of the line was Kerry Packer, Australia's richest man, bearing good tidings for his television network's most bankable personality. By way of a trip to Adelaide, Packer had secured for Martin and Channel Nine what would be the last television interview with Sir Donald Bradman.

In his 2010 memoir, *Ray: Stories of My Life*[1], Martin claimed that despite their enormous influence on the game in Australia, Packer and Bradman had never met. "Each man thought the other hated him," Martin wrote, "because of the war that erupted over Packer's World Series Cricket in the 1970s."

But when Packer and a mutual friend, Bob Mansfield, called in to Bradman's Holden Street address in Kensington Park, the meeting quickly became, in Mansfield's words

---

1   *Ray: Stories of My Life, Ray Martin (Penguin, 2010)*

to Martin, an "absolute bloody love-in". A deal was done too, for the interview to be accompanied by a $1 million telethon to help finish construction of the Bradman Museum in Bowral.

"So Kerry, how was it? Did you enjoy meeting The Don?" Martin asked.

"I loved it, son," Packer replied. "It was truly one of the greatest days of my life. He had answers for everything. Now listen, son. I promised him, when the show is cut and before we put it on air, he can have a look at it. I told him that if he doesn't like it, for any reason, then we'll burn the bastard. Okay? So don't fuck it up, son."

Martin and his production partner Peter Wynne duly travelled to Adelaide, and worked for two days with Bradman and his wife Jessie on the interviews that became the television special *Don Bradman, 87 Not Out*. Bradman never took up his option of final cut, and had no need to. It was a reverent piece of work, typical of the Bradman industry that expanded enormously around his legend in the 1990s. Martin tried to cover as much ground as possible, but like so many others before and since he left much unsaid and less understood.

Whether this was due to a quality the journalist Gideon Haigh has called "deferential incuriosity" around Bradman, or the overwhelming weight of preserving a visual document on the game's greatest batsman, Martin went over much familiar ground. He wasn't to know that in speaking to Bradman and Packer, he was a question or two away from a meeting of which little is known—well and truly a secret while both men were alive. Packer's enthusiasm for Bradman was genuine, but his depiction of their 'first meeting' was quite simply untrue.

Packer had none of Bradman's cricketing talent or knowledge, but his passion for the game—and its commercial potential—was unquestioned. Packer's involvement in the game—a grab for tightly held TV rights through 1976 and 1977—caused a revolution. Yet the two years of Packer's World Series Cricket breakaway gave rise to almost 40 years of coming together. Packer, Nine and cricket were to become synonymous, charting a path that the game is still bestriding. How that pathway came into being had as much to do with a secret meeting between Packer and Bradman, in Adelaide in February 1979, at the end of WSC's second season in Australia, as it did the bright floodlights of the SCG in November, 1979, when around 50,000 spectators crammed in to partake in Packer's re-imagined game.

What follows is a story that neither man particularly wanted told while they were alive. Bradman kept his direct dealings with Packer a strict secret, to the extent that he suggested strongly to one historian, Chris Harte, that he was pushed out of the way once the peace treaty between the ACB and Packer's Publishing and Broadcasting Limited (PBL) had been signed in mid-1979. To this day many cricket fans, and Ray Martin, have no idea that Bradman and Packer were anything but sworn enemies.

Packer, too, had an avowed preference for secrecy about his company and its dealings. There is a revealing anecdote in Damon Kitney's biography of Packer's son, James: on one occasion when Kitney was in the Consolidated Press building for lunch with his subject, the author was tersely instructed: "If Dad gets in the lift, you are not a fucking journalist, OK?"[2]

The intermingling story of two of Australia's most prominent, influential and private men of the 20th century remains fresh and intriguing even now, as we near the 40th anniversary of their first meeting. But it is not just a tale of Bradman and Packer. Far from it. The merging of sport and business—particularly with regards to the broadcasting rights money—and those rights' explosion in value over those four decades, has led cricket to places neither Packer nor Bradman could have conceived.

---

2   *The Price of Fortune*: The Untold Story of Being James Packer, Damon Kitney, (Harper Collins, 2018)

1

A trip to Adelaide

On 13 February, 1979, Kerry Packer rose earlier than usual, and drove out from his family's Bellevue Hill compound to Sydney's Kingsford Smith Airport. Boarding a Hawker Siddeley 125 private jet, Packer settled in for a journey shorter than most he had taken over the preceding two years. Rather than the Caribbean, London or the United States, the destination was Adelaide and an appointment with Sir Donald Bradman—a meeting that both parties hoped would broker peace at the end of the World Series Cricket "war".

Cricket's eyes and ears were uniformly elsewhere: Packer's WSC Australians, led by Ian Chappell, were en route to the West Indies, while the establishment side led by Graham Yallop was contemplating a 5-1 Ashes series margin from the glum vantage point of a rest day in Sydney. At that stage, thoughts of a compromise seemed far-fetched. In the considered opinion of *The Age* journalist Peter McFarline, who with Alan Shiell had broken the WSC story in 1977, the game's split would be enduring. "So the battle raged on," McFarline wrote in the closing passage of *A Testing Time,* his account of cricket's summer of 1978-79[3]. "It will do so, I believe, for some years yet, as both sides go their separate ways. And the game of cricket will continue to suffer injury."

Like so many others, McFarline reckoned without the power and influence of Bradman and Packer to shape the game according to their wills. Healing and deal-making were very much on the younger man's mind as the Hawker's pilot swung south-west, over the bushfires ravaging much of country New South Wales that day. Although he never admitted it to anyone but close confidants such as Tony Greig, Packer wanted to put out the WSC fire as much as anyone. It's not hard to imagine him, the jet closing in on Bradman's turf, muttering to himself that same phrase he'd offered Martin years later: Don't fuck it up.

Back in Sydney, at the Park Street headquarters of Packer's organisation, Lynton Taylor alone knew where his boss was headed. As managing director of WSC, Taylor was working assiduously at plans for WSC's third season, but also had hopes for news of a compromise. Taylor's

3   *A Testing Time,* Peter McFarline (Hutchison Australia, 1979)

TV career had begun in Adelaide, at the Seven Network. Once employed by Packer his role grew into the title of director of programming for the network, and then the manager of WSC. The cricket writer and historian David Frith, who met Taylor in early 1979, described him for *The Guardian*: "Solemn without being unpersonable, open-faced, forty-fiveish, quietly dressed, he speaks measuredly and stands for discipline, organisation in all he says and by his every gesture."

Taylor's first piece of cricket business had been conducted in early 1977, when he flew to London to secure the television rights for the Nine Network to that year's Ashes tour of England. In the days before his departure, Taylor had been aware of a half-formed idea on Packer's mind. "Kerry told me he'd been approached by Austin Robertson, John Cornell and Paul Hogan about doing a fundraising game for television either before or after each season," Taylor says. "Kerry was talking about it, wrestling with it, couldn't see how it could work or raise a lot of money.

"I flew to England late January, and had a cocktail party with the entire TCCB and members of the ICC. We started negotiations on the Tuesday, and I left on the Friday night with the rights. On the Thursday night Kerry rang and said, 'Son, I think I'm about to buy all the world's top players and start my own international series'. I said, 'Kerry, don't tell me that, I'm in the middle of these very tense negotiations and I don't want to know'. He said,

'All right, son', and hung up on me. I flew home to tell him we had the England series, and that's when I started to get involved in cricket."

That Ashes series would provide the backdrop to the discovery of Packer's plot some months later, and the journalists concerned, McFarline and the former South Australian batsman[4] Alan Shiell, were right in the thick of it. Shiell had been the first man outside the tight Packer circle to find out about the breakaway move, via his friendship with the Test team's newest star, David Hookes[5]. Shiell and Hookes had met for lunch at the Newmarket Hotel in Adelaide a few days before the 1977 squad's departure for England, and Shiell was to accompany them as a correspondent for *News Limited* Group. Hookes changed the tone of the afternoon when he let slip the biggest secret in the game, as much out of concern for his international future as a favour for Shiell ahead of his first overseas assignment.

"He was worried about his future and whether he'd be able to play Test cricket again," Shiell says. "He didn't think he would and was quite concerned. He didn't know for sure but he assumed everyone was in on it, but he wasn't completely comfortable. He was pretty happy about the

---

4   Shiell played 23 first-class matches for South Australia (1964-65 to 1966-67). He scored 1276 runs at an average of 33.57, with a top score of 202 not out against the MCC tourists at the Adelaide Oval in December 1965.

5   Shiell would be the ghost writer for Hookes' autobiography, *Hookesy* (ABC, 1993).

money, $25,000 a year, but the more it went on and the closer it got, the more he became worried about it and went to see Packer, who told him there was no way out of it.

"They all knew what it involved from the start—some might not have liked it, but they all knew they wouldn't be playing Test cricket. He would have been speaking to me as a friend too, chatting all about it knowing I wasn't going to write it the next day, but once it all broke he never had a go at me about it in England and was always comfortable about it there."

As a former player of some distinction for South Australia, Shiell's contacts among the players were impeccable. But his initial information was rebuffed by the *News Limited* chairman, Sir Kenneth May, when the pair met in Sydney at the insistence of Ron Boland, Shiell's editor at *The News* in Adelaide. "Oh, Kerry wouldn't do that, son," May told Shiell, before adding, "See what more you can find out over there and send the story through as soon as possible." No longer set to file the story before departure, Shiell became wary of the impressive connections built up by McFarline, an irascible and competitive correspondent. A few hours after his exchange with May, Shiell dined with McFarline at Sydney's Boulevard Hotel, with the pair both booked onto the same Qantas flight that would convey the Australian touring party to England. Although he had filed a broad story the previous October about televised cricket on Nine, McFarline needed more.

"Peter McFarline didn't know anything really until I told him that night at the Boulevard," Shiell recalls. "But there was that fear that because he knew so many officials like [Victoria Cricket Association secretary] David Richards and others, and because he used to get fed a few more stories than me, that he would drop it before me. So I thought it was better to take him into my confidence and that we'd both work together, so I was guaranteed it either way then."

Their resources duly pooled, the pair joined the team on the plane. In the early days of the trip both missed opportunities to follow up the story. McFarline, who died in 2002, recalled in *The Age* that several players, including the England fast bowler John Snow, greeted him with the words, "See you in Australia next summer", which seemed odd with India slated to tour. Equally, Shiell was either pre-occupied by celebrating their shared Anzac Day birthday with a drink or two with Gary Cosier, or snowed under by requests for other stories from the vast News Limited Group.

"It was strange in hindsight that I didn't ask much more about it immediately after I got to England, particularly not talking more about it to Greg Chappell, whom I'd roomed with for South Australia," he says. "But I was so bloody busy filing for the morning papers, the evening papers and the Sunday papers. Murdoch's Sydney papers weren't taking AAP then, so I was having to do the scores as well. I had *The Telegraph*, the Murdoch Sundays, *The*

News and *The Daily Mirror. The Tele* and *The Mirror* drove me mad."

So it was that the touring team and its attendant press pack reached Hove in Sussex, for the fourth match of the tour starting on Saturday, 7 May, with little to warn them of the storm about to break. At this point it seemed most likely that the WSC story would emerge from either Packer's own weekly magazine, *The Bulletin*, which was quietly preparing an official account of the venture for a June edition, with the insider knowledge that a formal letter outlining the breakaway would be delivered to the Australian Cricket Board within days. The respected English correspondent Ian Wooldridge was also on the trail and was taken into the confidence of Richie Benaud, Packer's prime consultant.

Wooldridge had called Benaud at his home in London, and initially received an evasive response. Some hours later Benaud called Wooldridge back with the words, "I think you'd better come around for a chat", leading to a comprehensive story to be published in *The Daily Mail*. Rain at Hove proved the catalyst for a more hectic turn of events.

After Greg Chappell and Craig Serjeant sought cover with the score 35 for one, Shiell wandered from the press area to a corporate tent, where he bumped into the business manager of the South African champion batsman Barry Richards, who had also played a season for South Australia in 1970-71. From that conversation Shiell learned that World Series Cricket was not just a domestic story, but had international implications.

Returning to the press corps, Shiell found that other conversations had taken place. "When I got back, an English journalist came to me and said, 'What do you know about an Australian TV mogul going to start up a rebel series in Australia'," Shiell says. "I pleaded innocence that I didn't know, and he replied, 'Wooldridge will have the story in on Monday'. Once I heard that I said to McFarline, 'We'll have to do it now for the Monday morning papers', so we went to see Greg Chappell after play had been called off early.

"When I told him what we had he had a funny look on his face and said, 'It sounds like an interesting proposition. I'd like to know more about it before committing myself'. McFarline had organised to go off to Tony Greig's for a party that night. McFarline went to the party and I went to the hotel and wrote what I knew. McFarline came back later that night, told me a bit more of what he'd been able to glean about more players being involved from other countries, and that was it.

"I still had time that Saturday night to ring the London bureau, and rang the story through to John Murche, who took it down and then put it on the telex to Sydney, for publication in *The Australian* and *The Daily Telegraph*. I wish I'd had a mobile phone or better phone connections then. I should've phoned Sydney. I should've phoned the sports editors to vouch for the story, but without that they weren't quite sure what to do with it. As it turned out it was on the front page of *The Australian*. *The Age* ran McFarline's story inside, and I'm not sure where the *Telegraph* ran it. It should've had bigger exposure, but in those days you didn't make unnecessary phone calls!"

While Shiell worried over whether the story would get its due, McFarline hatched a plan to ensure the joint venture was unique to their publications, inviting fellow reporters Brian Mossop (*The Sydney Morning Herald*) and Norm Tasker (*Sydney Sun*) to a Sunday morning round of golf that ensured they were out of range from their respective offices. Many years later, Mossop offers a wry chuckle when reminded of what had seemed a jovial offer to get away from the cricket for a few hours. "I knew bugger all about it, and it was actually suggested we should go have a game of golf on the Sunday morning," Mossop says. "So off I went to golf, and it was only when I got back that I discovered there was a flurry of speculation going around. Fortunately I had at least one friend among the cricketers, Ian Davis. I was sitting with Norm Tasker back at the Dudley Hotel when he [Davis] came over and said, 'Oh, dramatic events eh?', then unveiled what those events were.

"I ran off to find out whatever I could and it snowballed from there. I think I managed to get a Stop Press in *The Herald*, because by then it was pretty late at night, Australian time. I phoned the office and said this was going on and that was about the end of it for that night. Of course, all hell broke loose and then it was a case of filing stuff almost every day.

"I was surprised that Peter had gone to such lengths to keep me out of the way for the sake of a story—I suppose that's journalism for you. I wasn't amused, but there wasn't much I could do about it after the event. It was a big story and a bit of a pain to miss out on it. If I'd had a good day's golf it might have been a bit more acceptable!"

As Mossop, McFarline and Tasker sauntered around the links, Shiell took it upon himself to inform Australia's tour manager, Len Maddocks, and his assistant, Norm McMahon. "They didn't believe it and didn't want to believe it, but they soon had to believe it," he says. "That was the end of their comfortable trip. Things were never the same, on the tour or after it."

What followed was a bizarre few months for players, journalists and cricket fans across the globe. It was apparent that a cricket rebellion of this size, with the resources of major media company funding it, would change things irrevocably. For one thing, the usually comfortable relationship between the players and the press began to be eroded by a desire for further scoops. One Australian paper sent an investigative reporter to the tour, and he soon mucked in with the cricket correspondents. At collegiate dinners or pub meetings he had little to say, but then wrote several lengthy pieces about it all that appeared to be chapter and verse renderings of bar talk. The stories resulted in Mossop and others being harangued by their editors with cries of, "Why didn't you write that?" Yet full-time cricket writers had reasoned that much of this information would jeopardise an already febrile triangle between the press, the players and the tour management.

"Every day they wanted a political story apart from the cricket story," Shiell says. "There was a real undercurrent on the whole tour—you saw someone talking to someone else and you'd wonder what they were talking about. You felt sorry for the four guys who weren't involved—Kim Hughes, Gary Cosier, Geoff Dymock and Craig Serjeant. They felt left out when there were meetings among the players and they weren't involved. It just put pressure on everyone and hung over the entire tour."

Mossop's memories are similar: "The news was out, so one or two players were prepared to say a few things they previously had not admitted to, and as these things happen gradually bits come out and you get a whiff of something so you chase that. It was a fascinating time, apart from the fact I missed the first yarn. So having missed that it was a case of chase, chase, chase and make sure you didn't miss anything else.

"We had basically two tours going on from then on. We were writing about the tour we were on and writing about the tour to come—the breakup of cricket. It was split between those who had been approached and those who hadn't, and the atmosphere was different from a normal tour. It wasn't terribly antagonistic but some of the guys felt very left out."

Shiell recalls keenly the savagery of the criticism directed at the players, a trend started by Wooldridge's copy, which had been headlined, 'Cricketers Turn Pirates'. "Back then when cricketers were so terribly underpaid it was surely an accident waiting to happen," Shiell says. "And yet they got no sympathy at all in the press, particularly the English press who were really savage on them, but I'm sorry to say the Australian papers said much the same thing.

"They felt that Packer was a media competitor and treated the story as such. I was told certain things about how to tackle it. McFarline had a freer rein, whereas I couldn't be spared from the tour. I had to file scores every quarter of an hour at the county games. He stayed on for a little while after the tour and wrote *A Game Divided*, which was fair play to him because I was stuffed."

Shiell's sympathies were with the players. "So many players had given the game away prematurely because they couldn't afford it, and when you think about how far they've come now, 40 years on, it's terrible to think about how little sympathy the players got from anyone. No surprise how many players around the world jumped in on it."

Shiell and McFarline attended Packer's first press conference at Lord's after the venture became public. It was the scene of Packer's infamous declaration: "Now it's every man for himself and the devil take the hindmost".

Later, Shiell served as wicketkeeper in a press match, with Packer beside him at second slip. "At the end I had an offer to join some of the players and go to Amsterdam for a week to play some social games, all expenses paid, and I knocked it back. All I wanted to do was come home to see my son Brad, who was born in January 1976, so by September 1977 he was only one. Getting on that Qantas flight at Heathrow was one of the greatest feelings of my life, I tell you. That plane was a beautiful sight."

In recognition of five months' work without a day off and a share in the biggest story cricket had yet seen, Shiell was handed an envelope containing one extra week's pay, and then asked to get back into it, to cover the SANFL footy finals in Adelaide. "Difficult days they were," he says. "Difficult days."

2

A third season
is planned

As cricket wrestled with its new reality, Lynton Taylor did not exactly enjoy a smooth run himself. His role would change shape numerous times over the next two years, as the vagaries of cricket administration and broadcasting chewed up numerous Packer executives. The portrayal of a supine and intimidated "Gavin Warner" in the telemovie *Kerry Packer's War* did scant justice to Taylor, though it also hinted at the problems Packer had retaining a management team under highly pressured circumstances. General manager Vern Stone, administrator Brian Treasure and managing director Andrew Caro all came and went over the two years, amid a host of costly problems and submerged logs.

Caro took the blame for a messed-up run rate equation in the deciding final of the 1978-79 one-day competition, which had the West Indians and Australians at odds over the target Clive Lloyd's men had to chase at Waverley Park. A creeping 10.30pm curfew, as the West Indians closed in on 241 to win, resulted in frantic attempts from Caro and others to slow the stadium clock, then trying unsuccessfully to talk with the local council about extending the curfew by 15 minutes. Ultimately, the message reached Lloyd—but not Chappell—that West Indies needed 17 from the 46th over to surpass the Australian run rate. Lloyd and Joel Garner ransacked 18 from Max Walker's over, beginning at 10.28pm, and promptly ran off the ground in victory, accompanied by the umpires and an extremely agitated home team. Chappell's incandescent rage at Packer for this episode shocked teammates, while his offsider Rod Marsh was known to have repurposed the "C'mon Aussie, C'mon" jingle to express his distaste: a chorus of "Piss off Packer, Piss Off" showed the players' loyalty to WSC extended only so far as the bounds of the administration's competence.

For Taylor, Caro had been a source of discomfort for some time before that issue of run rates had reared: "He knew more about cricket than Richie Benaud, than the Board, than Kerry," Taylor says. "His ego was just extraordinary, but I was still chairman so I had overall responsibility for those first two years." When the Waverley match played out so unfavourably for the Australians, threatening to curdle relationships with Packer, it was Taylor who moved Caro on. "Ian made it quite clear to Kerry that it was unacceptable, and Kerry made that quite clear to me. Kerry came to me and said, 'Sack him'," Taylor says. "So I went into the Old Melbourne Hotel, caught up with him after the game and said, 'I'm sorry, you can't do that, as far as I'm concerned you're gone', and I had Kerry's imprimatur. He wasn't pleased about that but he went without any problems. That's when I took over not only as chairman but as managing director and took it forward from there."

Another lingering problem throughout the two years of World Series Cricket was the contractual status of Jeff Thomson, Lillee's much-vaunted new ball partner before the schism. Initially sticking with the establishment due to an existing contract, worth $633,000 over 10 years with the Brisbane radio station 4IP, Thomson decided between seasons to throw in his lot with Packer, but was unable to do so until the 1979 West Indies tour that followed the home season.

"We got Thommo back because he didn't play any games for WSC in Australia," Chappell says. "There was a great quote from Thommo when a journalist asked him why he wanted to go back (to WSC). He said, 'I want to go join my mates and the blokes who can catch'. I had a meeting with Kerry just before we flew to the Caribbean and he went through the Thomson saga, which was bloody hilarious. In the room there was me, then Austin Robertson, then Lynton Taylor, and then [lawyer] John Kitto. Kerry said to me, 'We've got Thommo, so you've got some fast bowlers to throw back at 'em son'.

"He's turned to Austin and said, 'Is fucking Thomson signed or not?' and Austin said, 'He's going on the tour, it's all fine', and Kerry replied, 'Is he fucking signed or not?' Austin then said, 'When I last spoke to Lynton, he said it was all fine', so Kerry turns to Lynton and says, 'Has fucking Thomson signed or not?' and Lynton said something or other. Kerry thumps the table and says, 'It's a fucking simple question: has he fucking put a pen to fucking paper yet?'

"So Lynton says, 'Well it's all sorted, I've spoken to the lawyers and everything's fine and [the law firm] Allen, Allen & Hemsley are fixing it', and he handballed it on to Kitto. So Kitto gets the, 'Is he fucking signed or isn't he?' and Kitto says, 'Well I've left it in the hands of [lawyer] Jim Thynne.' Then Kerry says, 'Where's fucking Thynne?' Kitto says, 'He's on holiday', and Kerry goes, 'Fucking where?' and Kitto says, 'He's on the Gold Coast', and Kerry says, 'Well I'll fuck that up', and he's gone bang and hit one of the buttons on his desk console and this voice says, 'Yes, Mr Packer', and all he says is, 'Get fucking Thynne', and I'm trying as hard as I can not to laugh as this thing got handballed down…"

Thomson would travel after all, but one legacy issue remained from Caro's desk after he had been "moved on"—the matter of tour payments for the Caribbean tour, whose first match would be played on 20 February, in Jamaica. Chappell, exhausted by the past two seasons and all that came with them, found he was now the middle man between WSC and the players.

"Andrew Caro had come to us (to discuss the West Indies tour) and said, 'We can't pay you the daily rate, because it's going to be very expensive and cost us a lot of money over there'," Chappell recalls. "We were there for eight weeks and I reckon it was $16,000, so $2000 a week—pretty good pay in the late 1970s. I said, 'That'll be fine'. Anyhow Lenny Pascoe and Ian Davis said, 'Nope, we want our daily rate'. With Lenny I said, 'What are you on about mate? I understand you signed a contract and all of that, but if you don't go, where are you going to get a job in Sydney for $2k a week? Where are you going to make $16k in eight weeks? Explain that to me'. Eventually Lenny was fine and he went."

When Packer and Taylor travelled to Barbados at the start of the tour, they did not expect the terse reception they would receive from the players. The scene said much about how weary Packer and Taylor were becoming about the business of cricket administration, as they tried simultaneously to get the Australian Cricket Board (ACB) and International Cricket Council (ICC) to the negotiating table. "We were going to lose money on the tour regardless, and he's made a unilateral decision to cut their salary," Taylor says of Caro. "I don't think the players were told until they got to the West Indies. Kerry and I got to the West Indies, to Barbados, and went into their room at the hotel. Kerry had no idea what was going to confront him and neither did I."

Chappell, having appealed for compromise on Packer's behalf, was to be taken aback by the extent to which the story of the contracts drew a reaction. Until, that is, he heard Packer's blunt summation of why the issue mattered. "I explained to Kerry there'd been this problem and it'd been sorted out, so then Kerry turned to Lynton and said, 'Aren't we fucking paying them what we fucking contracted them to?' And Lynton replied, 'No we're not'," Chappell says. "Kerry goes, 'Fuck, so how much will it cost us for them and the West Indies?' So Lynton's got on the calculator. It was $350,000 and I said, 'Kerry that's bloody ridiculous, the players are sorted', and he said, 'Fucking 350 grand? That's the price of a fucking B-grade movie, that won't break this fucking company. What will is not fucking sticking to our word. Fucking pay 'em'."

Season three plans had been across Taylor's desk for some weeks. In addition to the West Indies and the World XI, a full Pakistan team was mooted, and so too was a significant Indian contingent. Sunil Gavaskar's place in these talks has always been a matter for conjecture and Taylor confirms that India's captain had not only met him, but also facilitated talks with other Indian players. "We were going to have a fourth team," Taylor says. "We hadn't decided who that fourth team would be, but we had enough to have a full West Indian team, and enough for a full Pakistani team.

"I met with Sunil. He arranged for me to meet with others. Between them they were the six top players of the time in India, and basically we agreed terms and conditions for them to join us the following year. The likelihood is we would have had a Pakistani team included and then the World XI would be made up of the South Africans, the English and the Indians. That was the plan for year three—it was in place and agreements had been signed."

In *Gavaskar: India's Cricket God*, the author K.R. Wadhwaney quoted Gavaskar as saying that he would defect to WSC because it featured the world's best players, and that, "I am negotiating for better terms after my recent performances and I see no reason why I shouldn't get them." The Board of Control for Cricket in India (BCCI) responded by removing him from the captaincy for the 1979 tour of England, although he was reinstated in later years. Another senior player who reached terms with WSC, the wicketkeeper Syed Kirmani, was promptly dropped.

The status of the Indian players takes on greater importance when the ACB's tentative program for 1979-80 is considered: another visit by India following the relatively successful series of 1977-78. Had a compromise not been reached, the likely scenario was for a gutted official Indian touring party competing against a WSC fixture featuring Gavaskar and company. This was not a pretty prospect. Even uglier was the possibility of a series to ambush the 1979 World Cup scheduled for England. Australian and West Indies players were advised ahead of their Caribbean tour that they may be required for further cricket in England at a later date. Taylor did not rule out the option when asked about it in early February. "No such matter has been discussed formally," he told *The Guardian*, "but this does not mean that such a series is entirely out of the question."

Nevertheless, Packer and the Cricket Board had circled each other for some weeks. Talks with the ICC delegation of chairman David Clark, MCC and ICC secretary Jack Bailey, and MCC chairman Charles Palmer did not get far, as Taylor recalled:

"We worked endlessly to find a resolution with the ICC, the TCCB (England's Test and County Cricket Board) and the local authorities, but every time we were basically told to go and get stuffed. I held multiple discussions with the MCC and the ICC—very secretive, not necessarily in London or Australia. I met the ICC in New York, and it was obvious at the end of that meeting we were going to go absolutely nowhere with the ICC. I met with Jack Bailey at one point, so we tried every which way to try to get the ICC and the MCC to agree to some form of compromise, but none of it went anywhere.

"It got to a point where we didn't think there was any chance of getting a resolution that was worthwhile, unless we had somebody who really could bring some influence on Bob Parish and Ray Steele, because they were among our two major antagonists, supported very strongly by the TCCB, particularly its chairman Doug Insole, who was vehemently opposed to anything we did, and really didn't want to have anything to do with us." Packer could not understand why he was dealing with English administrators over what he saw as an Australian issue.

That led to a letter of approval from Palmer—then chairman of the MCC and ICC—for the ACB to speak unilaterally with Packer. At first Parish and Steele tried to negotiate, but existing enmity clouded a meeting with Taylor and John Cornell, one of the original organisers of the breakaway, and then Parish's next conversation with Packer. Parish's notes, reproduced in David Frith and Gideon Haigh's *Inside Story*[6], related a bullish exchange: "Money is no object and KP is certain he can buy the best of our players even if, in some instances, he may have to wait two or three years. Cricket is only three per cent of his business and the net profits of the company have increased yearly".

These words, in the context of driving for a hard bargain, didn't change the fact that others close to Packer could see the strain. One of those observers was Greg Chappell, who had returned the captaincy to his brother Ian when the breakaway began. "I have no doubt it was stretching

---

6   *Inside Story—unlocking Australian Cricket's archives.* Gideon Haigh and David Frith (Cricket Australia, 2007).

Kerry in various ways," he says. "I had a conversation with Kerry once—the fact of the matter is, it wasn't the money, it was the other things that were causing the problems. He had to spend money on programming anyway, and for a lot of the programming, to get Australian content, he would have had to pay a lot more than he was paying for the cricket, but it was a huge exercise in manpower and every other thing to run it and manage it, and I'm sure it was a huge strain.

"The strain was probably telling on both sides, and I know that financially it was telling on the Board as well. After the first year, they probably still had the upper hand, but the second year showed that momentum was turning away very quickly. But World Series Cricket had a finite life and one more year might have worked pretty well, but it could've been quite problematic after that."

It seemed there was only one way through the impasse, as Taylor noted: "Kerry realised that the only person who could have any influence over them was Don (Bradman), so he set about trying to find a way of talking to Don and he did that through Tim Caldwell, who was then the chairman of the NSW Cricket Association and a very senior member of the ACB Board. That's how it came about—Caldwell made the approach and Bradman was very eager to have a meeting. So it was arranged for a secret meeting at his home.

"Tim was the intermediary partly because we [the Packer organisation] were bankers with Bank of NSW and

Tim was a senior executive. I don't say he had sympathies, but he wanted to get it fixed. I have no idea whether he consulted with Parish and Steele, however we know he was the one who rang Bradman, he was the one who set the meeting up on strict condition that it was confidential and no-one was to know it was going to happen."

It was something of a gamble: no-one quite knew what Bradman might say. "We really had no idea where he stood, other than we knew he was the only one who could have any influence on Parish and Steele," Taylor says. "This all happened really quickly, it didn't happen over an extended period. Kerry was the only person who took part in the discussions with Caldwell to bring the meeting together, and he only confided in me after the meeting had been established. I assume his concern was if it didn't happen he'd have egg on his face.

"I think [secrecy] was crucial—up until we had concluded the deal it was highly secret from the TCCB, the ICC and other Boards around the world. Then Parish had to set about convincing them all that this was in the best interests of everyone, which was difficult with the TCCB. They railed against it. I think most of the other boards accepted this was the right way to go, but the TCCB were most certainly not on board with it easily."

Packer preluded his visit with an explanation of how he assessed cricket's value. "We have had a very high acceptance rate on television," he told the English cricket journalist Alan Lee in *A Pitch In Both Camps*[7], as the pair watched Australia's establishment XI collapse once more to Brearley's Englishmen in Sydney. "It has arrived. It's big, perhaps the best sports production on television—and that is what matters to me. The crowds at the ground are of secondary importance. Certainly it's great when they come, but it's television that counts. You see, if WSC can only break even over a season, then I have got 350 hours of TV programs for nothing. I've done well, haven't I!"

Critically, Packer also offered some of the most conciliatory words since the ICC blocked his television rights bid at Lord's in 1977. "I've always been willing to talk to anyone," he told Lee. "It's just that it's becoming harder to find anyone to have a chat with. To be honest, the compromise is not attractive to me now, and the longer it goes on the less attractive it will be. Why should I make the concessions? I am on a winner—it's the authorities who ought to be seeking the solutions now. I'm still prepared to do it for the good of the game, and I still say that if people of goodwill are prepared to sit down and talk with an open mind, there is an answer to this."

So Taylor waited patiently for Packer's return, in hope as much as expectation.

---

7   *A Pitch In Both Camps,* Alan Lee (Stanley Paul, 1979)

3

The Bradman Influence

Amid the rich gathering of Australian and English players assembled for the 1977 Centenary Test at the MCG, Sir Donald Bradman was the most sought after. Whether for photographs, conversations or autographs, he was the centre of an attention he had never quite enjoyed. No longer the chairman of the ACB, since his second term ended in 1972, but still its most influential voice, Bradman sat for much of the match with his English equivalent, Doug Insole.

At one point of a fluctuating duel between the teams led by Greg Chappell and Tony Greig, the hum of polite conversation was broken by Bradman's hushed but unmistakably rising tone. "Change places quick," Bradman said to Insole. "This so and so wants to sit next to me and I'm sure he wants to have his photograph taken and I can't stand him." The switch duly made, Insole sat and chatted with the would-be interlocutor until the lunch break, saving Bradman the trouble. It was not the first time nor the last that Insole saw Bradman's furtive nature, as he'd later reveal to the author Margaret Geddes. More than once Insole would write to Bradman upon the death of someone the pair had, he thought, both known. The reply to his pleasantries would often take an unexpected turn. "Well, not so sure about that," Bradman would write to Insole, "I mean he was all right, but I wouldn't trust him as far as I could chuck him."

It was in that state of secrecy, mistrust and often sharp judgment that Bradman bestrode Australian cricket's administration, virtually from the time of his playing retirement in 1948 until the breakout of World Series Cricket. In his time as an administrator he was most closely associated with two sagas, one very much on the field, and another concerning political discussions off it, and they are worth considering in an appraisal of his role in World Series Cricket. The first of those contretemps, in the late 1950s, was the matter of illegal bowling actions, a topic in which Bradman had taken a keen interest. Reversed film footage of Harold Larwood from the Bodyline summer, in fact, was to be one of his key party pieces in working, alongside English authorities, to rid the game of questionable bowling actions decades later.

The three major public players in the eradication

of throwing were Richie Benaud, the captain of the Australian team, Ian Meckiff, the left-armer with an action that had been hotly debated ever since he had run through England during the 1958-59 Ashes, and Colin Egar, the South Australian umpire who would be standing at square leg when Meckiff was recalled to the Test team to face South Africa in November, 1963. Each had critical exchanges with Bradman in the months leading up to that match, for which Meckiff had been chosen by a selection panel featuring Jack Ryder, Dudley Seddon, and Bradman himself. First, Bradman had hosted Benaud and the rest of his Australian team for dinner at his home during the fourth Test of the 1962-63 Ashes summer in Adelaide. Having screened numerous films of fast bowling actions, including the "mystery" left-armer who turned out to be Larwood in reverse, Bradman elicited from Benaud a resolution that should any bowler in his team be called for throwing, he would not recall him to the attack.

A few months later, in March, Egar was present for a SACA meeting at Adelaide Oval in which Bradman, he recalled to Margaret Geddes, "Explained to us the problem that was in cricket. And the administration wanted the help of all concerned to try and eradicate it." From that moment, Egar realised that, as an umpire, he could no longer, in his words, "leave it to somebody else", as the question of throwing was so complex as to have pitted country against country and now state against state. Later he would travel part of the journey from Adelaide to

Brisbane for the first Test with Bradman.

Lastly, during the tea break, after Egar had called the second, third, fifth and ninth deliveries in Meckiff's first over after lunch, causing Benaud to immediately withdraw him from the attack, Bradman approached Meckiff. "When all this has quietened down a bit," he said, "I'd like a word with you."[8] The word was to be had during the rest day of the match, in a conversation that stretched to two hours. Meckiff has recalled Bradman waxing philosophical about life, but getting down to the point that his cricketing career was over. "I think the best thing you can do, Mecky, is retire," he told the bowler. That is precisely what Meckiff did, retiring from all forms of the game at the end of the match. His public sacrifice, and Bradman's part in it, have been ruminated upon ever since.

Almost a decade later, the next crisis for Bradman and the ACB concerned the apartheid-era South African side, scheduled to tour in 1971-72. Australia had been the most recent team to tour the Republic, in 1969-70, as a last-minute change after Pakistan cancelled their invitation, to be replaced by Bill Lawry's team; the South African Board was expectant of a return tour. But it was Bradman's experience of the preceding winter's Springbok Rugby tour of Australia—complete with demonstrations and a major police presence—that helped convince him not to go ahead with the invitation for South Africa to

8   *The Summer Game*, Gideon Haigh (Text Publishing, 1997)

tour, as much as he wanted the tour.

As ACB chairman, Bradman had attended the Rugby international hosted by the SCG on 17 July, 1971, and spent much of the afternoon with the former Australian Test captain (and eventual SCG Trustee) Ian Craig. At close quarters, Craig observed Bradman's reactions to the demonstrations throughout the match and the police precautions, and heard his explanation of how much more difficult such a task would be for Test matches stretching to more than six hours of play over five days, with the likelihood of demonstrations. The prospect of smuggled mirrors being shone in the eyes of the batsmen in the middle was one such scenario Bradman raised, not only with Craig but also the police in attendance.

The union boycotts, barbed wire, the pits dug to extinguish smoke bombs, and interminable noise from protesters and police alike, left quite an impression. "It became clear as crystal," Bradman related later to the Board, "that it was a sheer, physical, utter impossibility to stage a cricket match under those circumstances. It literally couldn't be done."

Even so, Bradman was still mulling the possibility of the tour progressing when he met with the ACTU chief Bob Hawke, in a meeting in Adelaide—shades of what was to follow with Packer. Hawke recalled the critical exchange to Ashley Mallett, the Australian Test spinner turned cricket writer: "I went out to his home in Kensington Gardens," Hawke said, "and he said, 'Bob, I don't think politics should come into sport'. And I said, 'I couldn't agree with you more, Don. We haven't brought politics into sport; it is the government of South Africa which has brought politics into sport, because the government of South Africa has a policy that no person who isn't white is allowed to represent their country in sport. That's bringing politics into sport'. He looked at me for about 30 seconds and then he said, 'I've got no answer to that, Bob'."

This did not quite bring an end to the matter, as the Board continued to discuss the possibility of the tour throughout August. Its conclusion arrived in the shape of Bradman's dealings with the prime ministers of Australia and South Africa, Billy McMahon and B.J. (John) Vorster. As recalled by the former Board director Clem Jones: "Both prime ministers had expressed the view and the desire that the tour should not take place. Sir Donald expressed his views very forcefully that we must accept these advices but we must not be seen to be acting on the direction of government."

For Jones, whose Labor politics were very much at odds with the rest of the Board, the saga provided insight as to the kind of chairman, but also person, Bradman was. "Bradman was quite right-wing," he said in *Inside Story*. "He was the best chairman of any organisation I've had anything to do with, absolutely outstanding. But he was a bigoted, right-wing politician. People say he wasn't political: he was, and very much so."

According to most Bradman hagiographies, the events of 1979 took place when his days as an influencer were over. A succession of biographers have more or less ignored his role in WSC and the peace that followed. They speak of his declining health, his wish to withdraw from public life, and of his keeping out of "the Packer business". This extended beyond books to the accounts of numerous friends of Bradman, particularly those based in England. WSC had no more strident a critic than Insole, who in an assortment of roles with the TCCB and MCC made no secret of his distaste for Packer and his kind. In *Remembering Bradman*[9], Insole told Margaret Geddes: "The Don never really put his head above the parapet in the Packer thing. He was concerned I think—well I don't think, I know—about possible legal action as a member of the Board and although he was massively, vitriolically against, he didn't actually say so publicly. I think he saw himself as the pivotal figure, and that anything that he said would be massively more important than what anybody else said."

There was a rather more revealing tone struck in one of Bradman's last letters to Rohan Rivett, former editor of *The News* in Adelaide from 1951 to 1960. It was the 21-year old Rupert Murdoch's first masthead, and Rivett his first editor. In letters reproduced in *The Private Don*[10], Bradman wrote in the winter of 1977 that, "Packer's circus

9   *Remembering Bradman*, Margaret Geddes (Viking, 2003)
10 *The Private Don*, Christine Wallace (Allen & Unwin, 2007)

will fail". He went on to suggest a couple of editorial lines for Rivett to follow. "It is a pity that the whole truth of how well the players are doing cannot be told. One is not privy to the knowledge of the tax commissioner, but the stars like Lillee and co (who cry poor mouth) have undoubtedly been making enormous money by any standard." An encouragement to meet Bob Parish and be backgrounded on the Board's position was not followed up, for Rivett died in October, 1977.

Bradman's personal opposition to a professional game contributed to the curdling of numerous relationships. Apart from his oft-noted confrontations with Ian Chappell, there was the cooling of a longtime friendship with Richie Benaud, who had swung his considerable knowledge of cricket, broadcasting and commercial consulting behind WSC after Packer enlisted him to that multi-faceted role, at Chappell's suggestion. Benaud and Bradman had been close since they struck up a mutually beneficial friendship as captain and chairman of selectors, best summed up by their dialogue during the final tea break of the 1960 tied Test at the Gabba. When Benaud replied in the affirmative to Bradman's question about whether Australia was going to go for their final day target, despite the loss of early wickets, the chairman said: "I'm very glad to hear it." Seventeen years later another brief exchange took place when Benaud phoned Bradman to wish him a Merry Christmas for 1977. Bradman did not take kindly to the call and, after curtly saying he would pass the message on to his wife, Jesse, he hung up.

Greg Chappell also felt the ice of Bradman's displeasure during correspondence following the 1977 Ashes. The tour manager for that trip was the former Australia wicketkeeper and Board member Len Maddocks, who until his death in 2016 would remain deeply unhappy about the ructions created by the WSC split, and unsettled by the events of the '77 tour. Chappell charged Bradman with instructing the tour management to be as unhelpful as possible to the WSC members of the touring party. The following response duly arrived in Chappell's Brisbane letterbox: "Your own experience should make you realise," Bradman wrote in a letter published in *Greg Chappell: The Biography*[11], "that because of my prominence as an ex-player and administrator, the press sometimes tend to attribute matters to me when in fact I am in no way responsible and I am grossly misrepresented. This is a cross which unfortunately I've had to bear longer than you have been on this earth. It should obtain your understanding and not be used as a stick to beat me with."

Whatever Bradman thought of his own capacity to determine the course of events, it is not difficult to establish his true standing and influence at the time of the World Series split. He joined Parish and Caldwell as the three members of the ACB's "emergency committee", convened for sharper discussions when the unwieldy 14-man Board could not be summoned. "They", the

---

11 *Greg Chappell: The Biography*, Adrian McGregor (Collins, 1985)

former NSW administrator Bob Radford told Margaret Geddes, "were really the big three in Australian cricket". Bradman's word was seldom anything but the final one. Ian Chappell witnessed this at first hand when speaking to the Board on behalf of the Test team—even when he came armed with advice from Benaud.

"Particularly when it came to finance—that was where a lot of the problems started—it was as though we were asking him to spend his own money," Chappell recalls. "Also in a roundabout way it would have reflected on his reputation, because he was a big part of the finances. In 1973-74 we were playing New Zealand. I'd been to a Board meeting the year before, I think Tim Caldwell asked me to come along. I went along and spoke. Richie (Benaud) asked me how it went because he always said, 'I would've loved to have that opportunity when I was captain'. He asked how it went and this is rare for Richie but he said, 'If you don't mind a bit of advice, if you go again, write out your list of points, make 15 copies, one for each Board member and one for the secretary, and before you go into the meeting, put one on each spot, the list of topics. The reason I'm telling you is because if you just speak, they can put in or leave out whatever they want from the minutes. But if you've put it on paper, it should go in the minutes'.

"So next time I did that, and it was at Adelaide Oval, I went in, 14 sheets and one for Alan Barnes, the secretary. I'll never forget, points five and six were to do with finance.

I'm at the head of the table, Tim Caldwell was chairman, running the meeting, Bradman was sitting a couple places down on my right. Points one to four, Bradman sat back in his chair, I'd speak, Tim would ask, 'Anyone got anything to say? Right, next point Ian', and so on. I finished point four. 'Next point, Ian', and Bradman sat up in his chair. I spoke about point five. 'No son, we can't do that', then, 'Anybody else got anything to say? No'."

The disappointment and disillusionment Chappell felt was also due to he fact that he was aware of Bradman's own history of squabbles with the Board over his rights to earn money from activities related to the game—most notably by working as a writer. "That's why I was so pissed off with Bradman, because I knew from the family I came from, I knew about all those things," Chappell, a grandson of Bradman teammate, Vic Richardson, says. "So I mistakenly went into early meetings with him thinking that because of his history of fighting with the Board and particularly fighting with them over money that there'd be a bit of empathy there.

"But it wasn't empathy, it was the total opposite. I've described the meeting with him in his Pirie Steet office, to try to get the provident fund for SACA (South Australian Cricket Association) , walking out of there as like, 'Ian did you just walk in there, plonk your wallet on the table and say, 'Don, fill that up with money?' That's exactly how he made me feel."

This is not to say that Bradman's ideas were a source of

consternation or surprise *only* for the players. His fellow Board members could be confounded just the same. At the ACB's annual meeting in September, 1977, as the full force of Packer's legal and commercial machinery was crashing about the heads of the Board, Bradman spoke with a level of pragmatism that would have shocked Chappell. The minutes stated that Bradman, "felt that the Board should remain with the ABC for the next year, but that the time had come for discussions on the question of exclusive rights". Exactly what Packer wanted.

Pragmatism was central to Bradman's dealings over the next two years. He helped convince Bob Simpson to come back as captain of a weakened Australian XI, comparing the scenario to his own return after World War II. He also prevailed upon Ashley Mallett to play establishment cricket, before the off-spinner signed on belatedly with Packer. He worked shrewdly on the ground and finance committee of the South Australian Cricket Association to ensure SACA remained in reasonable shape, largely through the liberal use of Adelaide Oval as a rock concert venue. Meanwhile other states fared nowhere near as well: NSW had to sell its Cricket House headquarters.

Most surprising of all, at least to the Board, was that Bradman entertained discussions with WSC representatives about the use of Adelaide Oval, potentially with the installation of floodlights. Terms discussed included a $6000-a-day fee to use the ground on nine playing dates in late December, 1978, following on from the SCG's opening to Packer in May of that year. Journalist and cricket magazine editor Eric Beecher described this as "a little like Hitler asking Churchill for use of British airstrips during World War Two".

Ultimately those plans fell through, as, after the first season, WSC preferred programming matches in the more densely-populated eastern states. But the talks on the use of Adelaide Oval left the distinct impression that Bradman was someone who could be dealt with, and that he was not an establishment zealot willing to destroy the game in order to save it. Although he expressed harsh sentiments about the players and Packer to his friends, Bradman did not risk doing so publicly. Where many have interpreted this silence as a preference to not get involved, it was more like a case of keeping options open.

By then in his 70th year, Bradman was still quick enough on his feet to keep others guessing, as he demonstrated one night in early 1978 at the home of the longtime SACA medical officer, Don Beard. Before a dinner arranged for guests from the Australian and Indian teams, he took a bat, made his way down to the end of Beard's backyard net—a full length strip prepared by Adelaide Oval curator Les Burdett, and proceeded to play Jeff Thomson (bowling off a few yards) and others with characteristic precision. "To see these little feet dance down the wicket and go 'Bang!'," Rose Lill told Margaret Geddes, "It was extraordinary to see it, and he was thrilled to be doing it."

Ashley Mallett wrote Beard's biography[12]. In 2014 he told the *The Advertiser* of that moment: "… Thommo said, 'Well, if Bradman's batting, I'm bowling'. And Thommo said it was just the most amazing thing he's ever seen. For 20 minutes Bradman belted hell out of every ball. Didn't miss a ball. No box, no gloves, just the boys' bat and quite lively bowling. Thommo reckons he was bowling leg breaks but his leg breaks are about Dennis Lillee's pace, so they're quick. He was the quickest bowler who ever lived. Thommo said, 'I've seen a lot of old footage of Bradman and I thought the editors had knocked out all the bad shots but it was just—every ball, he smashed it. It was unbelievable'. It must have been an incredible thing to see, a bloke that age in horn-rimmed glasses and no gloves."

Within 12 months Bradman would be responsible for another bang—a shot heard round the world, and one that fundamentally changed Australian cricket. But it was not one he was to be publicly associated with.

12   *The Diggers' Doctor: The Fortunate Life of Col. Donald Beard AM, RFD, ED (Retd)* by Ashley Mallett (Wakefield Press, $32.95)

4

An extaordinary turnabout

I
t takes about half an hour to drive from Adelaide
Airport to the Bradman home at 2 Holden Street,
Kensington Park. What must Packer have been
thinking on that drive? As a cricket fan, he was about to
meet the greatest batsman of them all, but as a hard-nosed
businessman, he needed also to strike a deal. Packer's love
for sport was boundless and abiding, and he maintained
a sense of reverence for those who had represented
Australia. Asked once by Ray Martin whether he would
have "given anything" to play for Australia, Packer replied,
"Absolutely." Martin pressed further: "In what sport?"
Packer retorted: "Anything. Marbles."

So the vast figure who knocked at Bradman's front door was not just the major rival in a conflict that had torn the game asunder, he was a man with a deep love of sport and an admiration for its best practitioners. Packer also respected Bradman as a former employee of the family; it had been Robert Clyde Packer, the founder of the Packer empire, and Kerry's grandfather, who prevailed upon Bradman to give up a newspaper contract in order to avert his own confrontation with the Board and play for Australia during the Bodyline series.

Typically, guests at Holden Street were ushered into the front lounge room, with its decor little changed since the Bradmans took possession in 1934—an experience shared down the years by Bob Hawke, John Howard, Mark Taylor, Shane Warne and Sachin Tendulkar, among others. As Lady Jessie Bradman offered tea and biscuits, Bradman and Packer addressed their primary concern. Of the meeting, ACB minutes recorded simply: "February 13, 1979, Packer met Bradman in Adelaide." Benaud, Taylor and Parish have all offered fuller accounts.

Parish to Margaret Geddes: "When we did get to the stage of looking at a compromise, Mr Packer went across to Adelaide and spent about an hour with Don. When he came back I saw him [Packer] and he had a definite view that the ACB should control the game, provided he could get an agreement in regard to television. And not only television, he also got an agreement for Packer's marketing arm, PBL (Publishing and Broadcasting Ltd), to promote the game, and that's when the game changed."

Benaud gave his recollection to a lunch held at the Bradman Museum in 2013: "When he got down there, Kerry put it to Don that the cricket establishment should completely take over. There wasn't any doubt that World Series Cricket had won, Don said, 'That's correct', and Kerry said, 'I want to give back to you and the people you represent, every part of the game that we have at the moment, and I want you to run it as you always have done. I will have the television rights, which I've been trying to get for quite some time'. Don said, 'OK, there is a meeting of the board in three days' time. It will be done'."

Taylor recalls: "He flew to Adelaide early one morning, and met with the Don at home. Spent a couple of hours with him, but I think from the conversations I had with Kerry about the agreement to bring everything together took about five minutes, and the rest of it they talked about themselves, Bradman's history with the Packer family and everything else to do with cricket. Obviously, Sir Donald was keen to see the whole debacle come to an end.

"Kerry came back in the afternoon, having had four or five hours in Adelaide, and told me about the conversation. Whatever they agreed would only have been an agreement in principle to negotiate an understanding, because I'm fairly confident that nothing was taken back to the Board until there was a signed agreement, and then obviously it was a *fait accompli*.

It was a most extraordinary turnabout when the events of the previous two years are considered. Bradman and Packer acted well and truly in advance of public and press expectations and well before many on either side thought rapprochement was possible, though attempts had been made. Weeks later, as the rough outline of agreement was being fleshed out, Graham Yallop's bitterness as captain of the establishment XI was obvious, particularly when Pakistan's Asif Iqbal, who had played five WSC Supertests for the World XI before regaining his position in the establishment team for the official tour, arranged for Packer to visit the MCG for the first Test in March, 1979.

"Asif went on to offer his thoughts that a compromise was the only way for the Australian team to regain its status in international ranks in a hurry," Yallop wrote in *Lambs to the Slaughter*[13]. "Fair dinkum, who asked him for his words of propaganda anyway? That was a nice how-do-you-do on the eve of the Test in Melbourne. He was making a mockery of the official visit by his country to our country. He virtually manipulated a meeting between chiefs of the rival camps."

By the time Yallop's words were in print, the rival camps were no longer at loggerheads. Packer had left Bradman a month earlier with the assurance that cricket in Australia would be administered by the ACB, and Bradman left Packer with his guarantee that the deal for television

---

13   Lambs To The Slaughter, Graham Yallop (Outback Press, 1979)

rights and promotion of the game would not stumble at the Board table. The outcomes of that crowded hour at 2 Holden Street would reverberate for years afterwards.

5

A question of money

I n his dramatisation of the many theories surrounding the Kennedy assassination, Oliver Stone has his composite senior military figure, Mr X, utter the words: "That's the real question isn't it: why? The how and the who is just scenery for the public." The question of why Bradman accepted Packer's request for a meeting, and then promised to usher through whatever deal was subsequently reached, remains a source of wonderment to those who knew of the meeting at the time, or only discovered, many years later, that it had taken place.

The parlous financial affairs of the ACB and the State Associations must have been foremost in Bradman's thinking. The ACB's balance sheet for mid-1979 would show a $35,748 shortfall of liabilities over assets, which included 48 baggy green caps assigned a book value of just $648, to go with their symbolic depreciation in the eyes of the cricket public. The Australian coat of arms on the cap had undoubtedly been devalued, and it was to be a telling item of the subsequent deal that the emergent WSC logo was retained, if only on the breast of player shirts, as a lingering trademark of the breakaway era. All states had been pushed into varying positions of financial distress by the preceding two seasons—by a foe who not only possessed the money to outlast them, but also had the political and legal muscle to out-manoeuvre them.

Quite apart from the 1977 London High Court case that allowed WSC to go ahead on the basis of restraint of trade, Packer had caused plenty of anxiety among Board directors by securing the SCG and the Gabba to host matches in the second WSC season. Although the sight of the SCG being packed in November, 1978, made for great television pictures and a memorable sight for all who had witnessed it in person, its significance related as much to the power Packer had wielded. In encouraging the New South Wales Premier, Neville Wran, to replace the SCG Trust Board and install a new set of directors, Packer was able to stage matches in the establishment heartland—a welcome change of surroundings after the WSC troupe had endured the less attractive scenery of the Sydney Showgrounds. The combination of political influence and legal know-how caused, in the memory of Victorian administrator Bob Merriman, no small amount of consternation. "After he'd done the deal he did in Sydney people started to say, 'Hang on, woah'," Merriman says. "The fact that NSW Cricket didn't have that ground tied up so that he could get to use it was just bloody unbelievable. Parish and Steele had the MCG tied up so they (the WSC players) couldn't even walk on the ground."

Another plausible explanation for the haste of Packer and Bradman's accord is found in a theory advanced by Greg Chappell after conversations with the former Board chairman (1980-83) Phil Ridings. "Basically the Board lawyers told them that directors would be personally liable for any further costs," Chappell says. "Once they'd spent the Board's money and went into debt they would be liable for it. That was a catalyst for somebody, and I have a fair idea who, to speak to the Board chairman Bob Parish and say, 'You'd better get up to Sydney and have a talk to Kerry'. I heard that was the catalyst for saying, 'Let's just get this deal done, we don't need to be in this position'. Phil (Ridings) was very closely involved with the Board and with South Australian Cricket. He knew a lot of what went on behind the scenes and I'm led to believe that was a very strong catalyst for a certain individual on the Board to just get this thing done."

Chappell's theory is given credence by David Richards, whose knowledge of the Board's structure during his time as VCA secretary was such that, when appointed executive director in 1980, he would be given the task of reshaping the ACB into a fully incorporated body. Had the Board gone further into debt, Richards says, the liability would have fallen upon the State Associations. Of these, the SACA and the WACA, as ground managers at the Adelaide Oval and the WACA respectively, had most to lose because their substantial membership bases and subscriptions tied to ground admission went directly to each Association, whereas in NSW and Victoria the membership revenue streams from the SCG and MCC memberships flowed into the coffers of the SCG Trust and the Melbourne Cricket Club.

Given the link to memberships and ground ownership in SA and WA, there was the possibility, however remote, that Packer could have ended up not only having access to Adelaide Oval and the WACA Ground, but rights to the ground management. A SACA committee representative above all else, Bradman wouldn't be the man who sent the State Association and its members broke.

As a keen follower of politics and economics, Bradman knew of the potential for wider ructions, too. Looking beyond cricket's small economy, Australia was feeling the strain of a debate over how to tackle the next decade. In 1979 the national economy was only three years out of one recession and shortly to feel the effects of another, as the protectionist limitations on Australian business and industry ran up against a climbing import/export deficit, global trends of stagflation and the loss of former certainties about oil markets. This was the year of the

Shah's overthrow in Iran, hour-long queues for gas in the United States, and the US President Jimmy Carter's assertion of a "crisis of confidence" in the world's largest democracy. The partial opening of Australia to global markets, which would do wonders for the bank balance of Packer, among others, was still a matter for argument. Uncertainty etched itself on the faces of many more important men than the delegates to the Australian Cricket Board.

Knowing all of this, Bradman twisted from a position of staunch opposition to one of unqualified support for a new era, helping to rush through a peace treaty that gave Packer and Nine a rich controlling stake in the game for the next decade and more. Although the ACB did retain theoretical control of the fixture, the players and the running of the game, they would be compelled to cede enormous influence to Nine and its marketing arm, PBL. Exactly how much would become clearer once Packer's jet made its approach back into Sydney in the mid-afternoon after his meeting with Bradman.

6

Putting the pieces in place

5 4 Park Street is an address as synonymous with Packer as 2 Holden Street with Bradman. Packer's third-floor office was bedecked with paintings of an enormous bull elephant and a lion rampant, while an intercom system built into his desk gave Packer a line of communication to his businesses in Sydney and beyond. He would often host executives and other guests with his shoes off, and feet up on the desk, either grunting, bellowing or finding a register somewhere in between to manage the affairs of the day and deals of the future. The experience of waiting for Packer in the anteroom outside his office was enlivened by a third painting, of

dogs tearing a sheep to shreds. Sometimes this unsettling sight was accompanied by the sound of a verbal excoriation taking place on the other side of the door.

Taylor, though, was not to find his boss in that sort of mood upon his return from Adelaide. He remembers Packer recalling an exchange from the Bradman meeting that had Packer the dealmaker competing with Packer the cricket lover. After regaling Taylor with the story of the day itself, Packer got down to business, and to next steps.

"We'd come to an agreement in principle through that meeting to work through a full agreement as to how it would operate," Taylor recalls Packer's debrief. "But at that meeting (with Bradman) there were no details of how it would be constructed. All Bradman needed to do was to get his committee and then the full Board to agree that the discussions could take place and an agreement be reached.

"He (Packer) said to me, 'You're going to be our representative on this committee of five with Parish, Steele, Caldwell and Bradman. The only requirement I have is long-term television rights'. That was the last time Kerry had anything to do with the negotiations, because he then said to me, 'You've got to meet with Parish and Steele and get a deal done. I agreed, we've shaken hands,' and then he laid down four or five criteria that were essential to him."

These included the matter of finding a way to secure the rights to cricket in Australia, plus all matches played by the national team overseas, for a period beyond the kinds of short-term two or three-year deals that were commonplace. Some of Packer's other diktats included the handing over of administrative control to the ACB, and the splitting of revenue based on the idea that WSC—shortly to be renamed Publishing and Broadcasting Limited (PBL)—would promote the game in a way that was well beyond the capabilities of the Board. It was essential, too, that no WSC player be prejudiced in future selection discussions.

One early option had been to break up the season into establishment Test matches and floodlit WSC fixtures, with the ACB making its players available. "We did talk to them at one stage about having our own piece of summer," Taylor says. "In other words, we would clear all the players to play for their country except for this period where the Board would support a WSC competition, which would obviously only be one-dayers, because the Test matches would go on as normal. But that wasn't going to fly."

At this point Parish had grown doubtful of the possibility of a truce, but when he next met Taylor on 23 February, the impact of Bradman's discussions with Packer were made clear when Taylor offered to shut down all rival cricketing activity. After first stating that the ACB wished to regain control of running the game, Parish added that he felt it would be difficult to do so without a morass of legal issues ahead of 1979-80. His notes recorded Taylor's unexpected reply:

"LT appreciated the legal problems and then surprised

me by saying that they, too, believed that cricket would be better controlled and run by the various cricket Boards and that they believed that Test cricket should be the ultimate and with the current division the image of Test cricket could be irreparably damaged … Because of this, WSC were prepared to pay out all their players, honour all their obligations and close activities as cricket promotors. They would do this if the Board was prepared to enter into a long-term contract (say 10 years) to allow the WSC Channel Nine organisation to televise, market, arrange sponsors and generally promote ACB cricket."

So there, Parish had it, as had Bradman. Packer would allow cricket to return to its former custodians in exchange for an effective monopoly over its television and commercial affairs. Taylor worked busily with Packer's lawyer John Kitto to add detail to these basic terms, and by 28 February, 1979, had his proposal in a firm enough form to submit it to the Board's committee. Alongside Harry Chester, a senior company executive and mentor to Packer, Taylor met Parish, Steele, Caldwell and Bradman in Sydney, where the WSC/PBL "wishlist" was unveiled.

Here it is worth noting that Taylor remembers his proposal being pulled together as something of an ambit claim. His ideas for revenue-sharing included the appointment of PBL Marketing as the commercial agent for the ACB for a period of 10 years, with the option of another five, meaning that it would decide on broadcasting and sponsorship deals, among others. This created the scenario where a Packer-run company would decide who broadcast cricket on television in Australia, leaving all other potential bidders stymied in their attempts to pip Nine. The PBL/Nine monopoly would give rise to the quip within the ACB's offices that Taylor conducted subsequent negotiations "in the mirror".

There were to be guaranteed minimum amounts of money, drawn from gate and sponsorship revenue, passed on to the Board: $1.3 million for 1979-80, indexed to rise to $1.86 million by 1988-89. A little extra—$150,000 a season—was to be tipped in when cricket's profits did not reach a $1 million threshold. But any blue sky went to PBL, as did virtually all television advertising revenue, a figure that would swiftly advance into the many millions. Furthermore, the schedule demands were unrelenting: two touring teams per summer, up to six Test matches, and a minimum of 15 World Series Cup one-day games plus a best-of-five finals series.

If these terms sound harsh, Taylor stresses that he had expected some debate, some give and take. That there was none had a great deal to do with Bradman. "That meeting lasted about an hour and a half," Taylor says. "At that meeting I gave them a list of requirements, about a two- or three-page document, for us to settle. The meeting went backwards and forwards about what was likely to be agreed and what wasn't. I said, 'You have my conditions, it's up to you to consider'.

"At that point, Don said very succinctly, 'I don't care

what we have to give away to get this deal done, I want it done, as long as the ACB has control of the game'. Now that's not a very good thing to say at the first set of negotiations, but he was adamant that he wanted the deal done, it seemed he didn't care what they gave away to get the game back together. Pretty simple attitude, but typical of Don as I came to realise in the meetings I sat in subsequently with him after we'd done the deal.

"There is no doubt I knew then we could basically get what we wanted. So I didn't give in on anything, and that's why it's not something one would normally say. But he (Bradman) was doing it totally in good faith in the interests of cricket, and I still think the deal we did was in the interests of cricket. We did provide the Board with more income than they'd ever had before. What Don had said was key to that meeting, and it was key to the subsequent discussions."

For Bradman, the guaranteed minimums settled any doubts. The Board and the states would indeed have more money than they had ever seen before. This seemed a reasonable defence against the fluctuations of markets, and did not appear to tie the ACB to PBL's profits or lack thereof. For a career stockbroker who experienced his share of ups and downs in the market, as Bradman had, it made sense. In the words of Greg Chappell: "To be fair, he was a child of the 1920s, he'd been through the Depression, he'd seen what it had done to his family. I think that had a huge impact on the way he viewed the world from that point of view—you don't take risks. Cash is king and they had money in the bank."

But Bradman and the rest of the Board had very little idea of exactly how much money could be derived from a newly commercialised game. Nor did they particularly want to know. As Malcolm Gray, then a young director on the Board of the Victorian Cricket Association, and an occasional proxy to ACB meetings, observes: "Maybe unkindly, to a lot of those men $1 million was a lot of money, so if they're offered $5 million they think it's enormous ..."

A major absentee in the whole process was David Richards, one of few Board men Packer and Taylor had deemed capable. First employed by the Victorian Cricket Association as secretary, he had been involved in ACB subcommittees dealing with television rights while also helping to market the successful international summers of 1974-75 (Ashes) and 1975-76 (West Indies). He then won plaudits for helping to organise Melbourne's glittering 1977 Centenary Test and was, on the recommendation of Ian Chappell, approached more than once to join WSC during the war.

Instead, Richards continued to work assiduously for the VCA, and one January morning in 1979 he found himself shifting chairs in an MCG function room. While carrying one, he slipped over into another, cracking his sternum, and found himself on sick leave for six weeks. So, while early talks went on, Richards convalesced with his family in the Mornington Peninsula holiday town of Merricks. He had only the occasional phone conversation with Parish. "I was out of action for the whole of February and into early March," he says. "In that period I'm sure there were heavy negotiations going on between members of the Emergency Committee and Lynton Taylor in particular."

When Richards returned to work, the basics of the deal had already been settled, and he was not to have any influence over the fine print either. Instead he was immediately occupied by the task of organising the establishment's 1979 World Cup campaign, having been chosen as tour manager. Richards would get to know Taylor well, and believes his account of negotiations to be correct. "Lynton was a very good and capable businessman who would not give much ground in those circumstances," he says. "The bottom line is that the deal did mean all the states were better off than they had been previously. From the position we were in after the second season of WSC, it was understandable that they accepted the terms on offer."

In the West Indies, where a fractious WSC tour was staggering towards the last of a taxing fixture of 12 ODIs and five Supertests, Ian Chappell and his players were given a brief explanation: the rapprochement was about money. "We got a very brief precis of what happened and these were the reasons why," Chappell says. "As much as the Board had financial problems, also Kerry could see the money going out the door that fast...The stupid part about it was that the compromise probably occurred on both sides for the same reason—money. I know I've heard Richie (Benaud) say he wished WSC had gone one more season."

There were still a few hiccups before the deal evolved into a peace treaty. Government skepticism about the anti-competitive elements of the deal was to be the cause of numerous hurried visits to Canberra, and on 2 March, Caldwell related the concern of Chester that neither party should be taking "ANY RISKS AT ALL" in finalising matters. As it turned out, Packer's existing relationships with governments at state and federal levels were enough to smooth a path.

Allen, Allen & Hemsley's lawyer, Jim Thynne, whose holiday had been cut short by Packer over the contractual status of Jeff Thomson, was largely responsible for finding the fine-print solution. "We had legal advice on the 10-15 years, which was our original requirement with options," Taylor says. "The legal advice was, 'No, look there's no precedent, we're thinking that 10 years is the maximum you can get rights for in any one contract, so we then settled on 10 plus five with options."

All that remained was for the formalities: the documentation from Nine expressing interest in acquiring the television rights, and the ACB's response in acceptance. The new paradigm was to be summed up with some bitterness by Talbot Duckmanton, the ABC's General Manager and, to that point at least, an ally in the ACB's fight against Packer: "I asked for the opportunity to discuss our proposals further with the Board before a final decision was made to accept an offer from a commercial network," Duckmanton told his staff in a memo circulated around the public broadcaster. "I was not given that opportunity."

Among the more outlandish elements of the deal, the ABC was required to pay PBL a yearly fee of $1 million for the rights to broadcast cricket to regional areas that Packer's Nine Network could not reach. Duckmanton retired as general manager in 1982. One year later the ABC adopted Bradman's Test batting average as its Post Office Box number, 9994. Senior Packer executives had the occasional chuckle about that over at 54 Park Street.

7

Not making a bonanza

At the public announcement of the deal between the ACB and PBL Marketing, on 30 May, 1979, Lynton Taylor was asked to express his view about who had been the victor in the cricket war. "I don't think either side won," he said magnanimously. "I think the game of cricket won. It is peace with honour." Privately, Packer's lieutenants were far more triumphalist. For years afterwards, Tony Greig would tell friends that Packer's famed line—"you only get one Alan Bond in your life and I've had mine"—was not quite true: he had the ACB as well.

This was certainly the view of numerous other cricket nations, who were flabbergasted to read of a partnership struck only a matter of weeks after the two parties had seemed more opposed than ever. Any questions in the minds of Parish, Steele and the rest of the ACB about how smoothly this deal would play out were quickly put to rest by the reception the chairman, Parish, faced when he relayed its substance to the ICC in London, in June, during the World Cup. Thinking he would arrive to meet with an ICC that understood the game's predicament—and was aware of the ICC's letter of agreement to negotiate with Packer on behalf of the rest of the world—Parish received the shock of his administrative life. He related the drama in a letter to ACB secretary, Alan Barnes:

"I am writing this before I know whether or not the TCCB will agree to come to Australia (for the proposed 1979-80 Ashes series). I have never in my life as an administrator had a worse week. The attitude on Monday, 25th of June was one of veiled hostility … It appears that they did not inform the 18th June meeting that the ACB had acted unilaterally with the ICC's authority given to it by (Charles) Palmer."

Having cleared up this misunderstanding, and received "a complete change of attitude, and the expression of confidence in the ACB by every country in the room", Parish thought at first that his troubles had subsided. But this was to reckon without the TCCB, which remained strident in its opposition to a landscape shaped in any way by Packer, and still driven by the strong views of its most senior figure, Doug Insole. Parish was made aware of the TCCB's intransigence as he tried to put forward

Taylor's proposed schedule—a triangular one day series of 15 qualifying matches—between Australia, England and the West Indies with a best-of-five finals series was reduced to 12 and best-of-three after discussions with Parish. There was also to be a schedule of alternating Test matches, with Australia playing England and the West Indies three times each.

"This is the proposal that the TCCB is considering and will give a reply to me this morning," Steele wrote to Barnes, "otherwise England is off and India will replace them. This would be an absolute tragedy and would jeopardise international cricket relations for years to come. Frankly I am amazed and terribly disappointed at the complete lack of understanding, appreciation and co-operation."

After having had a relatively easy time of it with the West Indies, English cricket's custodians were in no mood for conciliation, led by their chairman George Mann. "It was immediately obvious that although the West Indies were prepared to co-operate program-wise, the TCCB was not. George Mann informed me that the unanimous view of his committee was that there was too much one-day cricket and that, in their opinion, this would denigrate Test cricket and have a serious effect on the welfare of the game and they considered it their responsibility not to agree to anything if they felt it could jeopardise the welfare of the game. There was no gesture of sympathy or understanding. In nearly four hours on 27 June at another meeting of the Test match playing countries I argued, publicly, with George Mann, whilst the other representatives listened in amazement."

As Taylor put it: "Doug Insole was vehemently opposed to WSC because he decided to instigate the bans on the players. He hated the deal and continued to express his repulsion at the deal the [Australian] Board had done with us. He was totally uncooperative with the Board and with me, and if there was anyone in England who carried the hatred of WSC, Kerry Packer, myself and anyone associated with it forward, through to the end of his tenure, it was Doug. He was absolutely, vehemently against everything we did. He wouldn't speak to me and I think he was having trouble speaking to Parish. During that period there were quite a few heated arguments with Insole, according to Parish, about the whole deal. It didn't stop with the signing of England to tour Australia that summer. Insole [England team manager that summer] was absolutely rude to Parish and Steele during that tour."

Eventually, the TCCB did agree to Parish's program, which featured a unique and never-repeated schedule of alternating Test matches with the West Indies and England, however, England would not be playing for the Ashes. The refusal to put the urn on the line in the three Tests summed up English resentment. Coloured clothing was another issue the TCCB opposed, leading to the bizarre initial sight of Australia and the West Indies being decked out in compromise uniforms that featured vestigial coloured piping on arms and legs. Not even that placated Insole or England's captain Mike Brearley, so England wore their traditional whites, their only concession a purely practical one: coloured pads in recognition of the white ball. Such traditionalism had been expected from Bradman, yet when Parish asked if he had any concerns with coloured uniforms, he responded: "Why should I? The pinks played the Blues in Sydney in 1892."

All this is to underline the greater administrative issue of the period: the TCCB was railing against a loss of control. *Wisden* noted acidly in the 1980 edition: "The feeling in many quarters was that when the Australian Board first found Packer at their throats, the rest of the cricket world had supported them to the hilt; even to the extent of highly expensive court cases which cricket could ill afford. Now, when it suited Australia, they had brushed their friends aside to meet their own ends."

Had *Wisden* editor Norman Preston or others known about a few of the clauses contained in the peace treaty, they may very well have stepped up their opposition. Tony Greig's son Mark wrote in *Tony Greig: Love, War and Cricket*[14] that while two years of WSC had cost the Packer organisation $34 million, this sum was comfortably recouped within the next two. Profits mounted even though PBL would be responsible for paying out fees to touring nations—figures that grew in accordance with

---

14 *Tony Greig: Love, War and Cricket: a family memoir,* Joyce Greig and Mark Greig (Macmillan, 2013)

the amount of cricket they were asked to play. Packer's fondness for the West Indies as a cricketing nation, and one whose Board had supported WSC, would would be reflected in future touring invitations: the best team in the world would spend time Down Under in six of the next 10 seasons.

"What nobody realises is we funded between 60-80 per cent of all the tours in those first ten years," Taylor says. "In other words, the West Indies wanted more money, the English wanted more money, and PBL put that money in so the Board didn't have to put it all up. Yes, we were getting a very good income from the rights we'd negotiated, but we did put an enormous amount of money back in to pay the teams that came to Australia."

England and the West Indies were paid tour fees in the region of $500,000 each for the summer of 1979-80. Richards, who, with Taylor, would take on most of the task of securing touring teams for the summers that followed, recalls: "I was taking a pragmatic view. This is the way the landscape was, and part of my job through my time with the ACB was to ensure we delivered the program of cricket we'd contracted to do. That varied from relatively easy to almost impossible, but it happened right through the period."

What Bradman and the Board had achieved through the peace negotiation was a deal that both guaranteed and limited the size of cricket as a business: although players would be better paid, there was a limit to what the ACB could pay them; although the ACB would grow over the next 10 years, it would remain a contained organisation, in which the Board and a small management group battled to contend with the growing demands of players and a decade of inflation while still seeking to build the game. Bradman and Packer were satisfied, others not so much.

As Bob Simpson, who in his 40s had come back from retirement to captain the establishment XI against India in the summer of 1977-78, told Margaret Geddes: "It was a revolution, but in the end it didn't go far enough. If you really look at it, the Board got what they wanted, control of the game, Packer got what he wanted, some of the senior players got what they wanted. But there were a lot of other blokes down the line on both sides who suddenly were saying, 'Hey, I thought we were going to be looked after'. Packer certainly honoured all his contracts, but they thought it was a lifetime thing."

Nothing summed up the mixed, muddled and rushed nature of the rapprochement more than the fact that a revolution supposedly based upon the need for the players to be better paid and have their own voice in the corridors of power ended without any players' collective body to speak of, other than a Board subcommittee that had already existed before WSC began. Its convenor was to be Bob Merriman, an industrial relations expert— later an Industrial Relations Commissioner—and cricket administrator from the Geelong region, who found himself managing the tour to India in late 1979 that was the last undertaken by a squad still shorn of WSC players. "Before the 1977 breakup they'd developed this cricket committee of the state captains," Merriman says. "Jim Higgs was on the tour to India, Kim Hughes as well[15], so Bob Parish decided to give me a full briefing before I went away on what the contract was, particularly as it pertained to the players, fairness to the players and what was going to happen. When we came back there was an anxiety to ensure the players got back together pretty quickly, and obviously the players with me in India were concerned about whether they were going to get a fair go and vice versa.

"Bob Parish asked me to consider a question of the players' committee. I had been talking with Ian Redpath, who I'd known for years, and the thought was put forward that we should get the WSC players together and get a sub-group from them to meet with Bob Parish and Ray Steele and Phil Ridings, because he'd taken over as chairman. So I met with Ian Chappell, Greg Chappell, Redpath, McCosker and Hookes in January 1980, at the Hilton Hotel in Melbourne, and the idea was to try to get a sub-committee out of that group to come and talk with the Board. Of course, Ian wasn't very happy about that. McCosker was prepared to be in it, Greg Chappell was prepared to be in it, so was Redpath.

---

15 The squad to India was, Kim Hughes (captain), Andrew Hildritch (vice-captain), Allan Border, Rick Darling, Graham Yallop, Graeme Wood, Dav Whatmore, Rodney Hogg, Graeme Porter, Alan Hurst, Geoff Dymock, Peter Sleep, Bruce Yardley, Jim Higgs and Kevin Wright.

"Ultimately what came out of that was when I went back and reported to Bob and Ray and Phil and David (Richards) that conversation, they amended the playing committee to be not just be state and Australian captains and broadened it. I encouraged the guys to participate. We used to meet in my office in Melbourne the night before we would meet with the three Board directors, Ridings, Parish and Steele. That became the cricket committee and we got quite a few things through like the then pension fund and a few other things that worked towards contracts, which came subsequently. Programming was a big discussion point."

This body's emergence contrasted with the curious fate of the Professional Cricketers' Association mooted by a bevy of the WSC players—the Chappells and Redpath in particular. Initially funded to the tune of $10,000 by Packer in 1977, its promising beginnings had stalled by the summer of 1979-80, and when Greg Chappell raised it with Parish in February, 1980, he was asked to make a formal submission to the Board. By the time of the June Board meeting, Chappell and Redpath had met with Parish, Steele and Len Maddocks, leaving Steele to conclude that "he was quite satisfied that the Board should not recognise the Professional Cricketers' Association."

Merriman's appointment at the same meeting as co-ordinator of the cricket sub-committee, which included players, deprived the nascent PCA of the one figure respected by both sides and capable of organising it.

While Merriman would go on to ensure the mending of various fences, a cricket sub-committee reporting to the Board was far less substantial, a token gesture rather than what the players had originally dreamt of—a body that had industrial strength. Having gained the television monopoly he wanted, Packer was not so fussed by players' rights anymore, and the Board seemed uninterested in the cricket sub-committee having any greater role than to help in the composition of a player disciplinary code.

At the same time, it was becoming apparent that they had bigger problems resulting from the peace treaty. As early as that same June, 1980 Board meeting, the first stirring of discontent could be heard, as the WACA director Bert Rigg pointed out in the ACB minutes: "The message that the Board was not making a 'bonanza' through the contract had not reached the public and players as much as was desirable." The payment marked down in the Board's accounts as coming from PBL specifically as the fee for Nine's TV coverage was a mere $250,000.

8

Chappell, I.M. vs Bradman, D.G.

I an Chappell's return to establishment ranks was typically eventful, resulting in a three-game suspension for abusive language towards an umpire during South Australia's match against Tasmania at Devonport. On his reinstatement he was to lead SA in its early-season tour match against Mike Brearley's Englishmen, and inadvertently bring an end to Bradman's time as an ACB director. "Howard 'Chops' Mutton was manager, and 'Chops' said to me, 'Ian, please promise me you won't swear at an umpire', and I said, 'I promise'," Chappell recalls. "So we then play the MCC and we must've batted first…"

By batting first, Chappell found himself facing two enemies at once: the young English all-rounder Ian Botham, fresh from his much-debated confrontation with Chappell two years earlier, when they were playing Melbourne club cricket for University and North Melbourne respectively, and the umpire Graham McLeod, a baseball clubmate of Chappell's who had set things up for a later confrontation. "Years before he'd come to me and said, 'I'm going to umpire cricket', and I said, 'Shit that'll be interesting, you don't know anything about the game'," Chappell says. "And he said, 'I'll fucking get you', and I said, 'I won't be worried about that because you won't be umpiring the games I play'. Then bugger me, he then became secretary of the Umpires' Association and appointed himself for the MCC game."

An early bouncer from Botham had Chappell turning his head and jogging a single after being struck on the back. A signal of "dead ball" drew an incredulous response. "I say, 'Turn it up mate, evasive action', and he (McLeod) said, 'No you just stood there and let it hit you', and I said, 'Well, one: why would I do that? And, two: if I'd done that it would've hit me elsewhere, I'll take my shirt off and show you the mark if you like', and I knew he was in trouble then because he changed his story and said, 'Oh it wasn't a bouncer', and I said, 'Mate I think I've seen enough to know one, it was a bouncer'. So I threw my hands in the air and let my bat fall. I go back down the other end, I know what's coming next ball and stupidly

I try to hook the shit out of it, gloved it—caught behind for nought. Botham told me to fuck off, but that's another story…"

Later in the match, after the visiting Englishmen had peppered the South Australian tail with short balls, Chappell's bowling spearhead Wayne Prior received a warning after one bouncer. "I didn't say anything at the time, but at tea time I went around to the umpire's room and it was Max O'Connell and McLeod," he says. "I said, 'I didn't realise there were two rule books here. How are they allowed to bowl three and four bouncers an over and we're only allowed one? I don't mind you warning Wayne Prior after one, but you've got to do the same for them'. McLeod must've said something and I said, 'Mate, you're incompetent, don't talk to me, I'm talking to Max', and that was important.

"Later on, I went down to fine leg to have a chat to Wayne and he had a long sleeve sweater. As I went past, instead of stopping and handing it to the umpire I just tossed it to him as I ran past to save a bit of time. I made sure I wasn't looking at McLeod but I made sure I knew where the sweater was going, and as I ran past I've gone 'voom', straight into his face and kept running. Next thing I hear: 'Come here, you', and Rowdy [Mallett] has walked across from gully and said, 'Why don't you just get back and umpire and leave him alone?' So, then I get hauled up. With the sweater, I told a little white lie saying I wasn't looking and just tossed it and didn't realise it hit him in the face, which I bloody did, but anyhow. But I also got hauled up for calling him a 'fucking incompetent'."

And who but Bradman to adjudicate on the matter? After all that had transpired over the preceding three years, and with a longstanding quarrel between Bradman, Chappell and his grandfather Vic Richardson, the touch paper was lit. Chappell, upon hearing that Bradman would hear the charge, made sure he was prepared. "I had to see Bradman down in the SACA rooms that used to be by the gates," he recalls. "So I've gone to George, the barman in the committee room, and he was a players' man. He'd quite often bring some jugs down because he knew we only got 12 bottles of beers, he'd say, 'The jokers up there haven't had this so you might as well', so he'd bring in these jugs of beer for us. I went up to George and said, 'What's the biggest glass you've got, grab it and fill it up with beer'. So I took this pint and lit up a cigar as well to go into this meeting with Bradman, because I knew that both would annoy the shit out of him, and I was at that point where it was anything I could do to annoy the shit out of him, or any other administrator.

"So we go into the meeting and he reads the charge and it's McLeod saying I called him a fucking incompetent. Again, I did this on purpose and said, 'That's crap', and I knew he wouldn't like that sort of language. 'I didn't use that language, I promised the manager, Howard Mutton, I wouldn't swear and I didn't. I called him incompetent, I'll admit to that, and that's not telling a lie, but I did not use the other word'. I got a six-week sentence, suspended for six months."

For Bradman, the need to deal with such old grudges and petty grievances, and the aftermath of his ruling on the Chappell incident felt like a signal to end his formal role at the ACB. "It was a set-up. The two other Board members cried off with feeble excuses and I had to sit alone in judgment," Bradman later told Chris Harte. "I heard the case; found Chappell guilty as charged, and suspended him forthwith for a period of six weeks. I sent my report to the Board, who did not back me up. Chappell's sentence was suspended. I had no other course of action than to see the season through and not re-nominate again."

Chappell, who retired from playing in May of 1980, notes the irony that he and Bradman saw themselves out of the top tiers of playing and administration within a few months of each other. But he was also struck by the careful tone of Bradman's disciplinary report. "Neil Blundell, the assistant secretary, was a bit of a fan and at some point, I think during that game, he walked into the Adelaide Oval dressing rooms and said, 'Ian, you probably should have a look at this, as soon as you're finished reading, bring it back to me', and it was Bradman's report.

"It was a typical Bradman letter, written in such a way that he made it very clear that he thought I was guilty, without actually saying that. There was nothing in the letter that was bang the table, 'this man's guilty', but you could tell from the way it was written that he thought

I was guilty. It was cleverly written so that nobody could come back to him. He never wanted to put himself in a position where people could say, 'Oh Bradman supported this or that'."

A dinner and lunch to mark Bradman's retirement from the Board were held in Melbourne at the commencement of the 1980-81 season, both events observed by Merriman: "We had the function for him, and he spoke very briefly. It was a dinner and then we had a nice luncheon the next day. I was fortunate to be there because Malcom Gray couldn't go, and that was my first Board meeting to make a report from the cricket committee, which used to take 15-20 minutes, then I'd be out. But this time because Malcolm was not there, I was in. A good one to go to. That night Don concentrated mainly on Lindwall and his 1948 people, which was fair enough. But he came around and spoke to all of us."

Gray, who had only just joined the Board himself and would soon be unseated by perceptions that, at 39, he was a mere upstart, can recall Bradman making him feel welcome. "I remember going to a Board meeting in Sydney as a proxy for somebody from Victoria in the late 1970s, and Bradman was on the Board. We broke for lunch and I was sitting there very much as the junior at the table, 20 years younger than everyone else and not knowing anyone, sitting by myself and it was Bradman who bothered to come over to me, sit down next to me and talk to me. That was the nice, gregarious sort of person.

Whereas at other times he was the dead opposite."

By the start of the 1980s, Bradman was happy to vacate the floor for others, at least in an office-bearing capacity. How much his dealings with Packer were influenced by a desire to end on the right note can only be guessed at, but whatever the truth, the discontents that followed were not to be Bradman's worry. He instead looked on from Adelaide, a phone call or letter away, making frequent trips to Adelaide Oval while remaining ever-present on the SACA's venerable ground and finance committee.

9

Doubling the workload

Greg Chappell has a simple way of summing up the change in the game over the Australian summers that followed—a recitation of how much cricket he found himself playing before, during and after WSC. In 1976-77, pre-WSC, he walked onto the field for 42 days of cricket, including two one-day matches. Wearing the WSC cap, he turned out for 44 and 43 days, with a far higher proportion of one-dayers (14 and 28). It was for this sort of summer's work that the players had been seeking a better deal in the first place.

"We weren't looking to become professional cricketers in the sense of playing cricket full-time," he says. "We still fully expected and probably wanted to have a career outside of cricket, but we just wanted a better return. When you're committing anywhere between six and nine months of the year to cricket, for a lot of the guys that was their sole income, so it was pretty tough. That's why blokes were finishing up in their mid- to late-20s, particularly if they had a family they just couldn't afford to keep doing it."

But when peace arrived, Chappell found himself confronted with a schedule that felt rather a lot like serving two masters. In 1979-80, his calendar featured 46 days of long-form cricket and 10 of one-day matches, a figure reduced by Australia's failure to qualify for the World Series Cup finals. Even so, back-to-back Tests was a concept learned the hard way: twice in 1979-80, two full Test matches were separated by the bare minimum of one day to travel from city to city. The following summer, Chappell found himself playing 62 days of Test and first-class cricket, plus no fewer than 18 one-day games; in the space of five seasons, his playing demands had effectively doubled, though the length of season itself had not.

"The first season after WSC we were playing alternate Test matches against West Indies and England," Chappell says. "Bruce Laird had his hand broken against the West Indies and couldn't play against England. We couldn't understand why England would get the benefit of what West Indies had done. We were playing Test matches intertwined with one-day games, there was no flow to the season, adjusting from one format to another. We played all the double-headers in the one-day matches—Saturday and Sunday we were playing two days in a row. It was hard enough from the playing point of view but exceedingly demanding from a captaincy point of view. Two one-day games in a row were physically and mentally more demanding than a Test match. The workload on key players was immense, and towards the end of a season they were pretty much exhausted."

Professionalism had hit Australia's cricketers hard. Where they once imagined themselves playing and practising more like golfers, they found the new deal to resemble that of a sweatshop, which just so happens to be a useful way of describing the MCG on Sunday, 1 February, 1981. Chappell's decision to direct his brother Trevor to bowl an underarm delivery to spoil any chance of a New Zealand victory has been dissected at length since, but it cannot be divorced from the explosion in the demands on Australia's cricketers. Chappell, a tired professional, and frustrated by the poor state of the MCG square, made a call designed to earn an extra day or two off for him and his team.

Those at the ground have recalled the selector Sam Loxton's tears at what had taken place, but it was Richie Benaud's excoriation of Chappell's captaincy that, via the Nine broadcast, has been seared into many more memories: "I think it was a disgraceful performance from a captain who got his sums wrong today, and I think it should never be permitted to happen again. We keep reading and hearing that the players are under a lot of pressure, and that they're tired and jaded and perhaps their judgment and skill is blunted. Perhaps they might advance that as an excuse for what happened out there today. Not with me they don't. I think it was a very poor performance, one of the worst things I have ever seen done on a cricket field. Goodnight."

It was to be Bradman, ears still ringing from those sentiments, who retired to his study at 2 Holden Street to hurriedly amend the World Series Cup playing conditions for the Board ahead of the next match of the finals series, to be played in Sydney—a favour, perhaps, for his fellow SACA committeeman and by then ACB chairman Phil Ridings. By the time Chappell had regained some small measure of public esteem by making 87 to guide his team home in the decisive fourth final on the Tuesday night, the prospect of any further underarms had been written out of existence in the World Series Cup playing conditions.

What had not, however, were PBL's scheduling demands, which came with the stinging knowledge for the ACB that every match under the minimum "15 preliminaries and five finals" World Series Cup model required the Board to pay a fee in recognition of the shortfall. After England had baulked at PBL's 15/5 outline for the previous season, the one-day tournament had been reduced to 12 qualifying matches and a best-of-three finals. The underarm incident came at the end of the first summer in which the 12/3 tournament was played.

Chappell's frustration with the program was clear. "As I tried to explain to them at the time, your business depends on us having a reasonable amount of success, and everything in the programming is working against us being successful over the long term," Chappell says. "We need to sit down and talk about how we can make it more equitable. The opposition teams were playing three Test matches and we were playing six. We were having problems with the MCG pitch—1977 was the last decent pitch I played on in my career at the MCG. It was just a mess for the next seven years.

"We were told, 'Oh well it's the same for all teams'. Well it's not because we play there twice as much as everyone else. 'Well you're making the same scores at the MCG as you're making elsewhere'. But you're missing the point: on a big ground like that, if we had a decent pitch we'd be making 50 per cent more runs on that ground than we would be elsewhere. You want to have something that's entertaining, and you're making us play on something that is very difficult to entertain on."

Chappell's meetings with Richards, Taylor, Ridings and others, whether as part of the cricket committee or solo as the national captain, seemed, to him, to go around in circles. What he interpreted to be a lack of interest in helping the players with their many complaints could now be seen as an inability on the Board's side to change many of the stipulations inked into the PBL peace treaty. And Chappell would reason that even if the players had taken a greater consulting role in the terms that were ultimately struck, they would have been doing so without genuine awareness of what lay ahead.

"I was meeting with David Richards on what almost seemed like a daily basis—very regularly. Every time I saw him we had discussions around those sorts of issues, and I got the distinct impression—not from David, who I thought genuinely tried to help us—there was an overhang of the old attitude that they're players, they should just get on with playing and we'll do the administering. They just didn't understand either before or after World Series Cricket that what they did had a huge impact on us. We certainly had more input, we had a players' committee, but I don't know how much influence we had on the big decisions. I think the smaller stuff, sure, but the deal had been done behind closed doors.

"We were in the West Indies and I think Kerry rang Ian (Chappell) at one time and had a chat to him about it, but that was the only real input that we had. I think it needed a lot more time and maybe that time wasn't available, that a decision had to be made. But I think having made the decision to get together, then I think they should have included the players in discussions. I'm not sure we would have avoided most of the problems, because it was only in hindsight once we started to experience some of it that we realised what the issues were. Once we realised, we really didn't have a mechanism by which we could talk to the Board and it was basically left up to me to try, one out, to talk to the Board *and* to Channel Nine."

Rather than pushing himself further, Chappell chose to partially withdraw. He resigned the post of selector handed to him as one of the terms of the peace treaty, and did not venture to England for the 1981 Ashes tour, heralding an unhappy period of shared captaincy with Kim Hughes, the establishment's choice as leader over the eminently capable but outspoken Rod Marsh. When he retired in 1984, Marsh remarked that he would have played on had he been given the chance to lead. He also remained adamant that his WSC affiliation had shunted him behind Hughes in the leadership stakes.

Marsh's duel with Hughes was emblematic of the fact that the ACB was fighting to maintain control of the game, in an environment where PBL, Lynton Taylor and his offsider Tony Skelton had an enormous amount of clout. The latter pair was aided by the fact that Richards was not inclined to push back; having worked at marketing the game himself, he was greatly impressed by the professionalism of PBL/Nine, and knew equally that the Board was a long way behind on that score. Richards also did not see the point in arguing against a deal that others had set in stone.

Incredibly, one of Richards' battles was to secure the ACB's rights to its own logo—the mirror image batsmen emblem dreamed up by PBL to complement the WSC ball and stumps. The marketeers' creeping influence was to be reflected in an attempt to gain control of junior cricket in Australia, a concept championed by Taylor and, on the Board side, Caldwell. Having served as link man between Packer and Bradman, Taylor now advocated a scheme whereby PBL would bankroll Australian youth programs, to the value of $300,000 per season. Then-prominent cricket coach Barry Knight, a mentor to Allan Border and a young James Packer, was put forward as a potential director. Taylor declared that PBL's intentions were as much about public relations as the identification of young Bradmans.

ACB minutes report Caldwell as saying, "He [Taylor] said that Mr Packer was concerned with his image in cricket and despite efforts to alter this was not succeeding. It was generally reported that everything that goes wrong with cricket was due to PBL influencing the ACB. If PBL were seen as good people behind the promotion of youth cricket, this may solve the problem."

Influenced by the opposition of a young executive in Graham Halbish, the Board filibustered the offer by referring it to various committees, before embarking upon its own sponsorship drives that led to a Barclays Bank deal for the Under-19 Championship, another with Australian Wool Corporation for the Under-17s, and The Dairy Corporation for Kanga Cricket, cricket's program for primary school kids. Merriman recalls that, given much of the recent fractured history at that time, there was a sense among Board directors that relinquishing their control of junior development would be a step too far away from direct control of the game.

"That was challenged very much by the fact we had Brian Taber and Alan Davidson from NSW, the same state as Caldwell, running Rothmans youth cricket arrangements as it was," Merriman says. "On top of that, Parish had spent a lot of Board money in Under-19s cricket, still supporting the schools, and ultimately we took that over. Then, of course, David Richards and Graham Halbish developed Kanga cricket first and then the Academy, whose first coach was 1964 Ashes squad member and Victorian batsman Jack Potter.

"What the Caldwell-Packer proposal did was to spark the Board into action: 'He's not going to take over any of our cricket, let's be as clear as on that'. We've just spent years over 'who owns the game?'—he owns the broadcasting, we own the game—and I think Tim probably came away from that Board meeting without too much support. It disappointed him, because he thought he was on a good winner, but he didn't even have support in his own state on that one, and there wasn't much seen of Tim after it."

It was the first time the ACB had successfully pushed back against the Packer organisation since the peace treaty had been struck. But there were to be more consequences of the deal to come: not as dramatic as the underarm incident, but far more damaging.

10

Command and control

B radman remained a fixture on the SACA's ground and finance committee until 1986, his 78th year, and, although many biographical accounts of Bradman draw him as a man in his dotage in this period, he continued to correspond with administrators around the country. His advice would often arrive unsolicited, but he made sure to stay in touch with the Board chairman of the day. As Col Egar told Margaret Geddes in *Remembering Bradman*:

"When I was chairman of the ACB between 1989 and 1992, even though he (Bradman) had ceased to be a trustee of [SACA], we still used to converse. I used to ring him up or he'd ring me and I'd say, 'But you must have heard this', and he'd say, 'Colin, nobody rings me up and tells me what's going on these days'. I'd say, 'Well okay, you've got a couple other people there [on the Board] whom you know'. 'No,' he'd say, 'I don't. That's why I want to have a chat with you, to keep my ear to the ground and see what's going on'."

Egar recalled attempts to expand Adelaide Oval in the 1980s, with an indoor centre and then what would, in 1989, become the Sir Donald Bradman Stand. Most of the time, Bradman's advice was summed up with four concise words: "Don't spend the money". In Western Australia, the WACA general manager John Rogers can remember receiving a letter from Bradman that contained a similar directive, amid discussions about the installation of lights at the WACA. Rogers wondered why things were still so financially tight in the age of professional cricket and its new revenue streams, and in early 1984 set himself to find out.

As part of their 10-year peace treaty with the ACB, PBL had just accepted Nine's renewal of cricket's television deal for another period of three years, but with the terms of the treaty kept secret from all but the smallest circle—ACB directors and Richards, Packer, Taylor and their legal teams. Few administrators knew exactly where the game stood. Working alongside the seasoned political advisor and investigative journalist Bill Mitchell, Rogers sought details of the deal, and at the same time researched the scope and value of television contracts elsewhere, particularly for Major League Baseball in the United States.

At the end of his and Mitchell's research, Rogers produced a report, in July 1984, titled *Three Proposals for the Advancement of Cricket in Australia*, which contained chilling findings for the ACB—so chilling, in fact, that there was considerable debate within the WACA about whether to actually pass the report on to the Board. Rogers estimated that Channel Nine/PBL had extracted somewhere in the region of $134 million in advertising revenue over the five years since the deal was struck between Packer and Bradman, yet the ACB had seen only about $2 million of that windfall. By way of comparison, the MLB and NFL had both negotiated five-year television deals in 1982-83, worth US$1.1 billion and US$2 billion respectively. The American leagues operated on a different scale, sure, but baseball's custodians received around 50 per cent of all money earned through television advertising during matches, much of which flowed through to the players.

Despite these findings, the status quo remained for the term of the deal, for reasons summed up by Richards: "There's no question because of the increased volume of cricket, the popularity of one-day cricket and day/night cricket, every state was much better off," he says. "It then became a moot point whether they could have been two times better off or four times better off—a waste of space as far as I was concerned. There was no point making an argument about it, the deal was done. It was set in stone for ten years and I think Australian cricket prospered. There was one time to sort it all out and that was at the end of the agreement, not before."

Merriman, who by now had become the Australian team manager, and had taken leave from his day job at the Industrial Relations Commission, agreed: "They did a deal under certain circumstances, when every state except Victoria was broke, and so they had to do the deal. In the circumstances, in my view, they did a very good deal. When you look at it ten years later, you look (at it) differently."

Even so, Rogers' little-known report deserves to sit alongside the Bodyline Cables and the Argus and Longstaff reviews among the vital documents in the story of Australian cricket. For the first time, administrators and Board directors were made aware of what the game was worth, and how television money had so dwarfed gate takings as a source of revenue. Just as significantly, they were shown the broad sweep of a trend that had left the ACB and State Associations increasingly reliant on handouts from PBL. Rogers' report concluded this was not just an issue of finances, but control:

> Directly, through its promotional role, PBL earns as much from the game as cricket itself. Separately, PBL interests have received TV rights for a peppercorn payment of one per cent of annual advertising revenue from cricket telecasts. On present trends, unless action is taken, PBL could be in effective control of top cricket before its

contract expires. The ACB has a duty to take action to acquire sufficient control over cricket's total earnings to be sure of effective future control over the game itself.

Never was the lopsided outcome of the ACB-PBL deal more evident than in early 1985. Kim Hughes's captaincy had imploded, after the second Test in Brisbane, leaving Allan Border to take on the top job most reluctantly. Despite facing one of the greatest sides to take the field in Clive Lloyd's West Indians, Border's team followed defeat in Adelaide with a scrambled draw in Melbourne, then a spin-inspired victory in Sydney, and a creditable display in the World Series Cup, losing the finals to the West Indies, two games to one. Just as Border seemed to be pulling a team together, and shortly before the start of an Ashes tour, the bombshell announcement of a rebel team to tour South Africa, a country barred from International cricket, spoiled all semblance of progress.

Each of the rebels was to be paid $200,000 after tax for two years of touring, far in advance of anything they could earn in official cricket. Hughes, Rodney Hogg, Geoff Lawson and others had grappled with the Board to seek improved player contracts ahead of the 1984 tour of the West Indies, and could not believe the repeated insistence of Richards and others that there was no more money available for the players once the states had taken their share. For players generally unencumbered by the political sensitivities, there was little hesitation to sit down with the entrepreneurial Dr Ali Bacher, the managing director of the South African Cricket Union.

When Packer and Taylor got wind of the tour, their response was instructive. Rather than working with the Board on a collective solution, they turned immediately to locking up players considered to possess the highest commercial value, while also safeguarding the future. Graeme Wood, Wayne Phillips (considered the most bankable batsmen after Border) and Dirk Wellham (an insurance option for the national captaincy), who had all signed on for the rebel tour, were approached. In *Cricket Rebels*[16], writers Chris Harte and Warwick Hadfield outlined the offer the players couldn't refuse: "The player's net earnings for the next two years would be deducted from $200,000, with the balance payable to him. Also there would be a minimum five years' employment with the Packer organisation, if it was required". Packer, having previously signed Wood for the non-existent third season of WSC and then having paid out the amounts owned under contract to all the others as promised, once observed to Ian Chappell: "I've fucking paid this bloke a lot of fucking money to never fucking strike a ball for me!"

Just as significant was the decision to sign up a handful of young players as a way of insulating them against South African overtures. After being talent-spotted by Tony Greig, each of Steve Waugh, Mike Veletta, Dean Jones, Robbie Kerr and Peter Clifford accepted PBL contracts worth $45,000 apiece in total over three seasons, each to be

---

16   *Cricket Rebels*, Chris Harte and Warwick Hadfield (QB Books, 1985).

managed by Packer confrere Austin Robertson, one of the original recruiters for WSC. For Waugh in particular, this deal and its underlying motive remained a strong memory. Even if the contract would buy him the land on which he built his first home, he never forgot the PBL bind, and ACB's parsimonious approach to player payments.

"They always cried poor, citing a need to look after grassroots cricket and saying they were paying us as much as they could afford," Waugh wrote of the ACB's approach in *Out Of My Comfort Zone*[17]. "Part of the story might have been true, but their financial situation was fairly and squarely their fault. Until 1994, when the ACB retook control of the game's marketing in Australia from PBL following a ridiculous deal struck in the early '80s, too much of the game's revenues were going straight into PBL's coffers."

Following the loss of the Ashes on the 1985 tour of England, news emerged that the number of South African defectors had increased still further. The South African-born Kepler Wessels agreed on terms to return to his homeland, after playing 24 Tests for Australia. A fixture in the Australian side since the 1982-83 Ashes series, Wessels would play one more Test before leaving Australia. Discussions around player contracts then intensifed, as related by Richards in his September 1985 report to the Board. Talks over two days with Taylor, then a delegation of players including Border, Andrew

---

17   *Out Of My Comfort Zone—the autobiography*, Steve Waugh (Penguin, 2005).

Hilditch and Lawson, plus the team manager Merriman, demonstrated the clear issue: PBL, having shelled out extra for the younger players of their choosing, was unwilling either to merge their own marketing contracts with the ACB's or to increase the pool of money available to players.

Richards' report to the Board summarised the meeting with PBL: "I met with Mr Lynton Taylor on Thursday, 19th September to discuss the allocation of key player funds and to see if he would increase the amount above our previously agreed $240,000 limit for 1985-86. Mr Taylor indicated that the key player agreements had been designed to retain the leading players by providing them with a base level of income. Because they had not been successful and because there were not that many leading players he felt needed to be retained, he had decided to reverse his earlier decision and would not now be contributing funds in excess of that contained in the main agreement. Although I argued the matter with him, he refused to change his views, and in so doing threw the plans for the following day's meeting with the senior players into disarray."

The players, still incensed by the way some among their cohort, such as Phillips and Wellham, had been rewarded for declining South African offers when others like Border and Lawson were stuck with the status quo, wanted stronger, simpler contracts with significantly better remuneration. Border, Lawson and Hilditch argued, with some justification, that "Packer thought it worthwhile to spend $225,000 over three years to save five young players for Australian cricket; therefore it has to be worth more than that to him to retain the best players". But even in the meeting itself, the divide PBL's hegemony had created was clear to see. Richards wrote:

"In answer to a question, Border and Hilditch indicated they would prefer to sign only one contract with the ACB and would be prepared to consider an offer embracing all rights including those in the area of private management. Lawson did not respond to the question—it is understood that he has a commercial arrangement with PBL which presumably is not dissimilar to the young player agreement."

The result of these discussions was that on 27 September, 1985, the Board's Executive Committee agreed—with the assent of Taylor—that a move be made towards combined Board contracts and PBL key player agreements, with the change to be funded in part by the $30,000 saved through terminating the marketing deals of the rebel players Kim Hughes, Rodney Hogg, John Dyson, Graham Yallop, Carl Rackemann, Tom Hogan, Rod McCurdy, John Maguire and Steve Smith. If the money to be earned by players in the future was to remain modest, it would at least be pooled together and directed to the players most deserving in the eyes of the Board and the selectors. By the following season, the ACB contract list now comprised most of the players who would lead the national team into more fruitful territory under Border's leadership. The annual retainers and guarantees for 1986-87, outlined in the ACB minutes, were:

Allan Border $36,000 - $55,000
Geoff Lawson $31,000 - $50,000
Wayne Phillips $21,750 - $35,250
Greg Ritchie $21,000 - $35,250
Craig McDermott, Andrew Hilditch,
    David Boon $20,250 - $34,500
Greg Matthews $20,250 - $34,000
Graeme Wood, Murray Bennett,
    Bob Holland $16,000 - $28,500
Dirk Wellham $16,000 - $25,000
Simon O'Donnell $13,000 - $25,500
Dave Gilbert $13,000 - $25,000
Ray Bright, David Hookes $8,000 - $17,500
Peter Clifford $8,000 - $16,000
Dean Jones, Robbie Kerr, Geoff Marsh,
    Bruce Reid $7,000 - $16,500
Steve Waugh $7,000 - $16,000
Simon Davis $5,000 - $8,500
Tim Zoehrer $5,000 - $8,000
Greg Dyer, Mike Veletta $4,500 - $8,000

Nevertheless, there was still a sense among the players that they were on their own. For a young Mark Taylor, who gained his place in the NSW team in 1985 as a result of Smith and Dyson's acceptance of South Africa deals, the landscape looked bleak. "There's no doubt we felt, looking back, that the one big mistake that had been made in previous generations of Australian sides was that off the back of World Series Cricket … the players then and there should have started something that was ongoing," he says. "I can recall vividly that we thought during that time that the big losers out of the game going back to the ACB and Kerry and Nine getting the TV rights was that the players had then gone back to where they were before World Series Cricket. Because there was nothing set in stone or no deal signed that looked after the players.

"So, to us, as big a driving force as out and out money was the idea that there was nothing in place to look after the players. To me it's one of the things I often reflect on. There's no doubt Kerry Packer was terrific for the game of cricket in almost forcing the world to embrace one-day cricket, night cricket and all those sorts of things. But the one thing we all found frustrating as players was that when he got the TV rights, which is what he always wanted, there was no legacy left for the players. Eventually through the ACA and (the pay dispute of) 1997, that changed and I think the legacy left by the Chappell era to us was that if you believed in something strongly enough, you stand up for it. That came out of it, and yes WSC did change the game, but it only changed the game for the players for those few years."

Seven years after re-unification, Bradman's main concerns were for what was taking place *on* the field. In the 1986 edition of *Wisden*, in an essay entitled *Whither cricket now?*, he wrote of accepting change and endorsing the one-day game—"especially day/night cricket"—while celebrating an audience that was younger and "liberally sprinkled with females". He also floated the possibility of line decisions being decided upon via television replays, the adoption of the existing one-day cricket restrictions for bouncers in all forms of the game, and the introduction of run-up limits for fast bowlers to aid over rates. Much to the surprise of many traditionalists, Bradman praised one-day cricket, and saved his major criticism of the game's modern era not for its commercialisation, nor its surfeit of white-ball games, but for the types of players now finding it hard to keep up. He wrote:

"It rids the game of the unutterable bore who thinks occupancy of the crease and his own personal aggrandisement are all that matter. It demands fieldsmen of great speed and agility with good throwing arms. The standard of fielding at all levels of cricket has undoubtedly been lifted. Running between the wickets, too, has taken on a new dimension. Risks must be taken to maintain the essential run-rate. Umpires are put under enormous pressure, having to adjudicate frequently on split-second issues: to their credit, I believe they have responded in a very positive manner and improved their standards."

He also addressed the issue of professionalism:

"The money now being paid to players has spawned professionalism beyond anything dreamed of 50 years ago. With so much money at stake I doubt if the modern professionals enjoy their cricket as much as did the players who were financially independent of the game and played purely for the love of it. Perhaps, too, monetary reward is responsible for some of the theatrical performances and even bad manners occasionally portrayed in recent years on the field. Happily I feel this unhealthy phase is on the wane, as players understand that good sportsmanship and keen competitiveness are not incompatible."

As an advocate of more adventurous play, Bradman offered this curt judgment when asked by the Australian sports journalist Phil Wilkins during the 1985 Adelaide Test about Sunil Gavaskar's achievement in passing his Test runs aggregate: "I am delighted to have witnessed Sunil's performance. He is a wonderful batsman, a player of rare gifts. But I would point out that while my runs were made in 52 Tests, Sunil's runs were made in a greater number of Tests."[18]

Sitting alongside Bradman in Adelaide whenever the cricket caravan passed through South Australia, Taylor felt that he continued to enjoy Bradman's *imprimatur*. "I do know from conversations I had with him when I used to go down to the cricket in Adelaide was that he was (a), very happy with the state of affairs and (b), he deplored the slowness that had crept into Test cricket, and he couldn't understand why it was the case—why there wasn't more aggression in the batting. He still believed the game was being played too slowly. He never gave up on

---

18 It took Gavaskar 80 Tests and 140 innings to pass Bradman's aggregate of 6,996 Test runs, a figure Bradman reached in 80 innings, across 52 Tests. After 52 Tests (95 innings) Gavaskar had 5,007 Test runs.

that. It was funny. He always thought the batsmen were too defensive. He was more than affable—he was very pleased with the way the game progressed."

Bradman's thoughts certainly appear to have influenced Lynton Taylor's frequent requests to the Board to change playing conditions, with suggestions as varied as changing limited overs over limits from 10 overs each for five bowlers to 10 for one and eight for five more, and advocacy of the use of lights to extend Test match playing days. The introduction of bonuses and penalties for overs bowled above/below the mandatory 90 in a Test match day was another recurring suggestion, while the gap between ODIs and Tests was addressed by the recommendation that separate selection panels be appointed, with the limited overs selectors to be notably younger and of more recent experience than the Test panel.

But by the end of the 1985-86 season, Taylor's suggestions were becoming increasingly like directives, and Taylor's eyes were on the fact that the initial ten years of the ACB/PBL peace treaty were nearly up, and it would soon be time to negotiate renewal for a further five years. Taylor had every reason to believe that, with the Australian team struggling and the ACB still wrestling with itself, PBL Marketing held all the aces.

11

'Two dead horses'

I f there was a moment that summed up the oddness
of PBL Marketing's deal with the ACB, it was
Lynton Taylor's contention in a newspaper interview
in January, 1982, that "the game of Test cricket as it's
presently constructed is archaic", and that "I don't know
that Test cricket can be saved". Attempts by the Board
to wring an apology or clarification from Taylor were
unsuccessful. "He did not intend to denigrate the game,"
Taylor was minuted as telling the Board's executive
committee at its 27 March, 1982 meeting, "but stated that
people were not prepared to spend five days watching a
cricket match."

These views only hardened with time, becoming still
more strident at the end of the 1984-85 season. In an

address to the Board on 19 April, 1985 at the WACA ground, a matter of days after it was revealed that 16 players had signed to tour South Africa, Taylor made it clear where he felt the blame for these defections lay: "It is disappointing to come before you today with problems of such magnitude besetting the Board. For the second time in a decade, the Board has lost a multitude of players to a competitive promoter of the game of cricket— why? I do not intend to delve deeply into those reasons in my speech today, suffice to say that the comments of the players and the response from the Board to my company's suggestions to assist in a material way, lead me to the conclusion that the lessons of 1977 have not been learnt.

"Last year, I complained about suggestions from PBL Marketing being treated in a pre-emptive way, that as partners it would be polite, if nothing more, that before rejecting out of hand our recommendations and delivering us a prepared Board position, we were invited to participate in discussion and allowed to be part of the decision-making process. I had understood that this was accepted until the events of Wednesday. Individually, I have a respect for every member here today. Collectively, however, your decision-making process does no service to cricket."

He went on to shift blame for average daily attendances of 14,000 for the summer's Test series against the West Indies to the poor performance of the national team: "During the season I read a number of articles discussing the reasons for the lower than expected attendances and the performance of the Australian team hardly rated a mention. I read that the prices were too high, the promotion not strong enough, the weather too hot and a few other assorted reasons. Even Kim Hughes, when captain, was reported as saying that the team's performance did not affect the attendance. Well, nothing is further from the truth. A one-sided contest with the national team performing badly is of little interest to the Australian public, as our research in Adelaide immediately after the Test match showed.

"Listen to what the public gave as their reasons for not attending, "no longer any excitement" - 31%, "it was a foregone conclusion" - 38%, "Australian team performed badly" - 52%. This is a normally supportive public, disillusioned with their team. All other factors pale into insignificance when the national team loses its credibility."

Still more bullish was Taylor's next address to the Board, in April, 1986. Speaking at length about the future, the ACB and PBL's relationship, and the television landscape for cricket, Taylor imparted a message that verged on the dictatorial. Its substance leaves little doubt as to how Taylor felt, while his message that the PBL deal to the ACB, "has also allowed, through guaranteed financial support, contractual arrangements with players to provide some protection from overseas interests seeking to arrange cricket tours" rang somewhat hollow, delivered as it was a couple of months after the completion of the first of two rebel tours by Australian teams to South Africa.

The first portion of Taylor's pitch for renewal related to Benson and Hedges, cricket's major sponsor at the time: "They, more than anyone else I would suggest, have an interest in knowing if PBL, the Nine Network and the ACB will continue to work together. Forward planning is essential for them, firstly due to the very substantial funds now involved, and secondly because of the influential role we have forged for cricket in their national marketing strategy and product positioning. They require high-profile national commercial television coverage to justify their level of spending and they deserve to know if PBL Marketing and the Nine Network will be maintaining their involvement.

"There is no way the Benson and Hedges Company can support even its current level of sponsorship without the commercial television exposure and national marketing support that we provide. Unless they can be offered an assurance that your future intentions will protect them, then you are merely inviting them to look elsewhere for opportunities. It is in your interest to extend their sponsorship at the earliest possible time, thus providing for a valuable sponsor immediate protection from vexatious legislation brought by either state or federal authorities.

"It hardly needs underlining that such legislation would also restrict your Board's future options. We do not believe any commercial alternative exists at the level of funding provided by the Benson and Hedges Company. The breweries, which currently are so active, are not up to the same spending levels and the next group of prospective sponsors are well below them in available money."

Having addressed sponsorship, Taylor turned to Nine's television coverage over the past seven seasons, specifically its high standard, and then lobbed the grenade that it had come to his attention that efforts were being made to look elsewhere. "It was with a certain amount of shock then that the Nine Network was recently told that agents—other than PBL—acting for the Australian Cricket Board, have been sounding out the ABC and Channels Seven and Ten on whether they would be prepared to televise cricket after 1988-89. I will leave it to you gentlemen to rationalise the loyalty aspect of such a happening, all I will say is I found the news mildly astonishing.

"It has meant that the network now has suddenly been forced, as a protective measure, to become interested in local and international sporting contracts which shortly come up for re-negotiation and, in addition, wonder if I did the right thing in having PBL reject overtures from organisations such as the Victorian Football League, the Confederation of Australian Motor Sport and the World Heavyweight Title fight in Perth in order to fulfil our obligations to cricket. Those and others would have been joint Nine/PBL promotions.

"No television network can afford to sit around to wait and see if those resources mentioned earlier are going to be utilised. They must plan ahead to ensure full productivity is maintained. There is a real danger, in the absence of a forward schedule, that these facilities will be committed to other events and Australian cricket will suffer the same fate as English cricket, which has lost its priority ranking and nowadays has to share its telecast hours with other sports and events."

Driving his point home, Taylor painted an unpromising picture of cricket's global stocks, before adding a kicker to his claims of disloyalty: PBL Marketing could not sustain its current resources for cricket without knowing what the future held beyond the next two years. "Those commercial elements which have worked so well and which we have worked so hard to maintain must be re-negotiated over the next 12 months," he said. "Part of our role is to point out, as I am today, that cricket's commercial future needs to be protected. Six months from now, that commercial future will have become increasingly uncertain. Not that we haven't enough problems on which to concentrate without entering into protracted negotiations."

Taylor's 1982 critique of Test cricket's uncertain future now became a roaring criticism of the way the ACB had ignored trends. "Several years ago I was accused of becoming alarmist when I raised concern regarding the future of Test cricket and for that I suffered derision in some quarters. I wonder if I appear so out-of-touch now. The problems that were evident to me then are growing.

"There is a rapidly ageing audience for Test cricket with little inducement to attract the casual supporter or the young. In a recent Sydney survey less than seven per cent of people under 25 planned to attend Test matches, the lowest figure yet recorded. To think when I first voiced my concern, preference for Test cricket had dropped to 14 per cent. Is it any wonder that the daily attendance at the Tests last season was under 9,500? And what in five years has the ACB done about it? Well, I'm still waiting to have that meeting to discuss the matter.

"During the season, I was interested to hear of media and committee meetings concerning the Sheffield Shield. If the purpose of such activity is to revive spectator interest in the Shield then you are flogging a dead horse and while you are doing that, you are overlooking the sick but not yet terminal animal called Test cricket. Unless you are prepared to divert your attention, you will end up with two dead horses.

"Do not listen to the argument about too much one-day cricket—one-day cricket reflects the social attitudes and priorities of this quadrant of the 20th century. No amount of committee discussion will alter that. Do not think that by reducing the number of one-day matches you will divert the public to Test cricket. They will just find non-cricket activities in line with all the varied personal requirements and interests of modern day people."

With an emphasis on ticket prices, Taylor swerved to attack the "mutterings" he was aware of from the Board about the PBL deal. "It worries me that it is not the consumer acceptance or otherwise which is at the heart of this concern but rather the fear that PBL Marketing makes too much money. Do we?

"Over the last three years—three pretty good financial years for cricket—our average share of gate receipts has been $1.67 million and the ACB's share, $2.82 million, nothing like the 50/50 split members of the Board are so fond of quoting. While I listen to your complaints regarding the increased operating costs of cricket, the costs of cricket marketing aren't getting cheaper either, not to mention the team guarantees, the player payments, the media and the many other benefits we provide to the Board. Any additional revenue we receive from gate receipts will be quickly eaten up by the forecast increases.

"Our share of the teams' guarantees alone for next season is budgeted in excess of $1 million. In fact, team guarantees have cost PBL Marketing some $4 million over the course of our agreement. These are escalating costs which the Board, at the moment, does not have to share. It would be impossible to maintain the current standard and level of cricket marketing without obtaining an increase in revenue and I would be surprised if the ACB can maintain its operation either. So when you examine the pricing levels, examine them on the standard of public acceptability, not on whether PBL Marketing stands to gain what you mutter about being an unfair advantage."

After showing the Board's advertising plans for the coming summer's Ashes series, and remarking on the favourable financial prospects for 1986-87 in light of the rivalry with England, Taylor returned to hammer home his message: Test cricket was in trouble, and any prevarication over extension of the PBL deal would serve only to exacerbate the issues confronting the long form of the game. "With the extent of our support and a reasonably confident prognosis of another good financial result from the season, the Board may succumb to the temptation of putting off the hard decisions which need to be made about Test cricket and about us," Taylor said. "Well, gentlemen, you have run out of time on both issues. Test cricket is suffering from its lack of public appeal now. The five-year warning period we have given you has elapsed and you probably have a one season's respite with Test cricket's best drawcard—the Ashes—and then no amount of rhetoric or newspaper columns which live in the past will be able to hide its decline. I believe you must inject positive innovation now.

"As for our agreement, I have watched with some detachment the Board's decision-making process and from time to time made my opinion known. I have no intention of having the time and effort of either myself or my executives chewed up by that process. We should be in a position to lay down agreed principles by the start of this season and by its conclusion we should have at least come to a consensus on which to base a Heads of Agreement. If we are unable to reach an agreement or the discussions drift on without conclusion, then we will take it there will be no continuation and commence our forward planning accordingly.

"I trust this is a step we do not need to take. While a number of cricket's senior administrators have had difficult digesting our involvement, I believe that our association has been both fruitful and positive for the game and under the right circumstances, we can continue to work jointly to secure cricket's future as Australia's No.1 national sport."

As the ACB directors picked up their jaws from the floor, Taylor reiterated his previous ideas regarding bonuses and penalties for Test match over rates, and spreading the load of overs required to bowl in ODIs. Finally, he concluded: "I don't believe it is the Board's responsibility to guard the past but rather it is to protect the future of the game. This should mean a studious and cautious approach to change, but an approach nevertheless. An approach which has been missing for several years, but an approach you cannot delay much longer."

Taylor's address, until now hidden from public view, was another strong ambit claim from a hard-nosed businessman, in line with his pitch at the end of the WSC war. In 1979, with the ACB and the states on the verge of bankruptcy, Bradman and the rest of the emergency committee were compelled to accept Taylor's view of the world. But by 1986, even with the significant setbacks being faced by the Board, things were not quite so bad that acceptance was again the only option. Besides, the directors, including younger blood such as Alan Crompton (NSW) and Malcolm Gray (Victoria), were growing wiser as to the commercial potential of Australian sport.

"We found Lynton Taylor difficult to deal with," Crompton told the writer Christian Ryan in *Golden Boy*. "Nice guy socially but a bit overbearing, a bit bombastic. Bullying, yes, I think he tried to bully us. PBL tried to have more influence than they actually had. I think we hosed them down."

The ACB was helped by the manner in which wider events in the Packer universe took the corporation's focus away from cricket—namely, efforts to deregulate the Australian television market that led to Packer's sale of Nine to Alan Bond in the midst of the 1986-87 summer. Packer's wealth had grown unabated as he purchased vast tracts of property in country NSW and the Northern Territory while living an increasingly extravagant lifestyle. It was amid this period of empire building, and following the deregulation of the financial system as Prime Minister Bob Hawke and his treasurer Paul Keating opened up the Australian economy, that Packer sold Nine to Alan Bond for an unprecedented $1.05 billion.

First, however, the Board's direction would shift via a change in chairman: the 70-year-old New South Welshman Fred Bennett, having presided over four remarkably fractious years and showing signs of strain, was replaced in October, 1986 by a younger, more aggressively business-minded figure, the 46-year-old Gray. He was to push a far more strident line in dealing with PBL, aided undoubtedly by Bond's emergence as a suitor for the Nine Network.

"I always said why *not* deal with Packer?" Gray recalls of the journey from the ABC to Nine. "I could see no reason why cricket should have to stay with the ABC…all of that was just driven by history and tradition, there was no other reason. It was ridiculous.

"I was concerned as well that sporting administrators didn't understand or know the value of sporting rights. A lot different from today—this is 30 or 40 years ago, and people were in sport in positions of influence or power, on state Association Boards or national Associations, and in the 1980s and 1990s they'd be offered money for rights which was say 50 per cent more than they were getting previously, and they say, 'Oh this is fantastic'. They really had no idea what they were getting, and in fact I always believed they were getting undersold.

"That goes right back to the ABC—the ABC was a crook deal. It was all a slow process, and I think all along there was a view—certainly I had a view—that PBL was getting a far better deal than cricket was. It is true that cricket was seeing more money, but it goes back to my questions: How much did we really know? What was the value? With a two-party agreement, how do you know what's reasonable? What's 50/50? I certainly had a view that it wasn't 50/50 all along, going back to the early 1980s. One might've had that view, but it doesn't mean you could do much about it. That *was* the deal. And there was also the fact of, 'Why are you carrying on? We're getting more money than we used to, we're doing pretty well…'"

Upon his appointment as chairman, Gray spoke publicly and strongly to talk up his product, with a confidence befitting the chief executive of Gray Johnson, one of Melbourne's largest commercial real estate firms. He told sports journalist Greg Baum in *The Sun* on 1 October, 1986: "Cricket has dealt with the problems of change over the last decade better than any other sport or organisation. It has coped with professionalism, both in terms of the sport becoming professional and its administration becoming professional. It has coped financially and economically with the booms and the recessions. It has coped with the advent of private enterprise. The ACB, through PBL and its sponsors, now has a very good relationship with private enterprise. And it has coped with the international scene well. We had problems with South Africa last year. South Africa was a major crisis in sport. We lost 16 players, or one and a half teams, 25 per cent of the national competition, and we've coped with that."

Part of the coping mechanisms included the appointment of full-time support staff for the national team, in the form of the coach Bob Simpson (who would fill that role between 1986 and 1996) and the physiotherapist Errol Alcott (1984-2006). Both proved their worth early on during the 1986 three-Test tour of India, where the tied Test at Madras was followed by two draws. Australia still hadn't won a Test series since 1984, but the way the team stood up in demanding foreign conditions, against an Indian team that had enjoyed much the better of the previous home summer's 0-0 stalemate, offered the promise of more to come.

Even as the Ashes loomed, Gray's forthright views about the PBL deal were becoming more widely known. Says Merriman: "Malcolm Gray, becoming ACB chairman, did not like in any way, shape or form, the deal that had been done with Packer, particularly the marketing, and particularly the gate. He couldn't see any reason why they (PBL) should be getting a percentage of the gate. He couldn't see any reason why we weren't doing our own marketing."

What followed was a gradual hardening of the ACB's position towards Taylor, as charted over the course of several Board meetings. On their own the minutes of those meetings tell a subtle tale; added to the fact that Border's men were in the process of being overwhelmed by Mike Gatting's English tourists, the prevarication to delay Taylor negotiating on his preferred terms starts to look something like heroism from the ACB.

The ACB minutes, from 5 December, 1986: "It was agreed that the chief executive should meet with Mr Taylor and convey in detail the Board's views, which in summary were that the Board would be prepared to consider any offer PBL Marketing wished to make, provided that there were changes regarding accountability and disclosure."

The minutes from 6 January, 1987: "The chief executive reported that following the December executive committee meeting, he had again met with Mr Lynton

Taylor and reiterated the Board's statement of principles. Mr Taylor had agreed to put forward a proposal in time for consideration at the February executive committee meeting."

At that meeting, coach Simpson offered up his frank assessment of the national team, and the system supporting it. His words were to lead to a significant change—Simpson was to become a selector, with the 1987 World Cup in India and Pakistan to be among the first teams he had a direct say in choosing. Doubtless, too, Simpson reassured the Board by indicating that he would not be agitating for more money for the players. "He reported that the players have worked very hard in practice sessions and their disappointing match results (the Ashes were lost 2-1) were not a reflection of lack of endeavour," the Board minutes stated. "He was concerned regarding players lacking knowledge of some of the basic skills of cricket, including poor concentration, and recommended an end of season meeting of state coaches to tackle this problem.

"He felt there should be more emphasis on the diagnosis of a player's mistakes and also suggested there should be better co-operation between state and national selectors so that Australian players are better utilised in state matches. In a wide-ranging discussion, Mr Simpson commented that there had been a breakdown of peer influence of senior players coaching younger players; that players did not have a very good understanding of their professional responsibilities as full-time cricketers; and that the question of remuneration was not contributing to players' anxiety levels about future security."

Having been revitalised on the field by a win in the fifth and final Test in Sydney, the news of Packer's sale to Bond was also met by the Board with considerable optimism, giving it the *chutzpah* to reject Taylor's offer. By the time of a 4 February, 1987 meeting in Devonport, Gray's Board was dictating terms—though to whom they were not quite sure: "The chief executive reported in full on his memo of 27 January, which detailed the proposal received from PBL Marketing. After considerable discussion on the alternative courses of action, Mr Bennett moved, Mr Pettigrew seconded that the chief executive advise Mr Taylor that the Board cannot accept the offer; that the Board reiterates its wish to enter into one or more television rights agreements direct with the television networks; that it is prepared to discuss with the Nine Network the rights position through 1994 in the first instance; and that in view of the recent acquisition of Channels GTV9 and TCN9 by the Bond Corporation, to ascertain who is authorised to negotiate on behalf of the network now."

The wait was not a long one. By March, the Board welcomed the arrival of a new man to address them: Jim Fitzmaurice. The sale of Nine hurtled Packer into multi-billionaires' row, but also took him and Taylor momentarily away from cricket. In the meantime, as

Bradman advised Egar, cricket needed something more than money to remain in good health: "The player must have an inner commitment, apart from the money. There is a great danger of the dollar being such a dominant factor that it erodes the underlying integrity and purpose of the sport. It behoves all of us to realise we are custodians of the welfare of cricket and must guard its future even more zealously than its present."

In ways that Bradman had not foreseen as necessary, the ACB was about to set out upon the task of doing just that.

12

A New Bond

Kerry Packer's withdrawal from the ownership of Nine seems only ever to have been temporary. As related by the journalist Paul Barry, Packer told the *Herald and Weekly Times* group managing director John D'Arcy: "Sport, first I'm going to take three years off and get fit. Then I'm going to come back and buy television stations for half the price their new owners just paid for them. Then, son, I'm going to have some fun." At the time, however, there was enormous shock within Nine at his decision. Network promos, injecting new life into the "Still The One" marketing catchphrase first picked up in the early 1980s, now looked to be as pleading as they were boastful.

The man entrusted with calming the nerves of many

of the network's stars, not least their cricket commentary team of Richie Benaud, Tony Greig, Bill Lawry and Ian Chappell, was Jim Fitzmaurice. Having built a grand reputation as a broadcaster in his own right for the ABC in Perth, Fitzmaurice also recruited and mentored a young Dennis Cometti—eventually to become an Australian sports broadcasting luminary—and was partly responsible for the polished but entertaining style Cometti would make so distinctive over the following decades. "The ABC was a bit stiff in those days and I probably broke the mould a bit," Fitzmaurice says. "Because I injected a reasonable amount of humour into my broadcasting, but not to the point where I felt it was interfering with the main story. Particularly with cricket there is an odd opportunity to talk about something other than the cricket."

As had David Richards, Fitzmaurice rejected several entreaties to join World Series Cricket between 1977 and 1979, but was well aware of the player discontent that was at the heart of the split. "They compared themselves with other professional sportsmen, and you sensed that among the players, they were in a mood where they just wanted change," he says. "I remember this group in particular talking about golfers, one of them (Rod Marsh) had a brother, Graham, who was a prominent golfer, so you'd be able to work out who he was! He made the point that look at what my brother gets for the skills he's got and look what I get—an interesting comparison." A move into management with the ABC led Fitzmaurice to PBL

Marketing in the early 1980s, where he can remember Packer's tendency to delegate detail: "Some project was coming up, and I think I asked him a question about 'what do you think?', and he said, 'Listen son, that's why I employ you'." Granted that sort of latitude, Fitzmaurice rose in time to be the executive best positioned to replace Taylor in early 1987, and his Perth connections, particularly with the Bond organisation, helped.

"I was probably a bit different because, although I wasn't born in Western Australia I spent a lot of my early years there and started my broadcasting career in WA," he says. "Alan Bond came from Perth, and Warren Jones was a key player at the time, as chairman of Bond Media. I'd known Warren from way back and he knew me, and most of the people associated with the then Bond Media I knew well, so to me it was no big change. In some ways I quite looked forward to a situation where I would work with Warren.

"But it generally caused amazement that the deal was done and that Kerry had walked away with a deal he hadn't expected to get. I can remember having to talk to a lot of our talent about the fact that Packer may have gone but things aren't going to change and we'll continue in much the same vein and so forth. There was potential there for some individuals to think that without Kerry it wasn't going to be the same and maybe they'd look at their options. But none of that happened and I thought the changeover worked quite smoothly. Nine continued to operate as it had been and, if anything, it got bigger and better."

There was a rather different emotion, something like relief, that Fitzmaurice experienced in his initial meetings with the ACB. No longer dealing with Packer and Taylor, the Board believed it could now flex a little more muscle in the knowledge that under Bond, Nine was trying to retain a sense of continuity—and nothing was now more emblematic of the network than its coverage of Australian cricket. To that end, Fitzmaurice believed as much in strengthening relations as he did with wringing cash out of any deal; the two, he felt, went hand in hand.

"What my sense was, and they didn't leave me in any doubt about it, that the relationship with Nine/PBL had not been great. I got that message loud and clear," he recalls. "Effectively the Nine Network or Packer, whoever you want to talk about, effectively had a very strong grip of the game. Then you got to the point where there was that transition. And I really came in at the point where my direct involvement was in the Bond years when the scene was changing. Looking back on it, I always felt the major role I was trying to perform at that time was one of PR. You had to step fairly carefully, but at the same time you had to cling to a certain level of professionalism that you didn't want to see wiped away.

"I felt there were some potential wounds that had to be healed, and I also felt looking at it from the point of view of the organisation I was working for, that I wanted to cement relations in a way that it wouldn't just be a one-off quick hit of association, but that it would develop into something longer-lasting. That's always the case when you're doing those deals, you've got to make sure that you've got a good working relationship. I was aware there was unhappiness, but in those circumstances you think, 'Well the past is interesting, but this is what I've got in front of me, let's get on and do it'."

Partly due to John Rogers' report, and partly due to the upheaval created by the rebel tours, Australian cricket was growing wiser about its circumstances and how they needed to change. Malcolm Gray, speaking in *Inside Story*, said that amateur administrators of Bradman's era were finally having to see things as they were, and to work intelligently towards more favourable terms:

"The deal that had been struck [between Cricket and PBL] was a very poor deal, commercially naive, inept, done under extreme duress. No doubt about it," Gray said. "And it was a deal that if you'd started with a clean sheet of paper and equal power on both sides of the table, you'd never do. I'd get exasperated by people carrying on about what terrible people they [PBL] were, and how they wouldn't tell us this or that. A lot of the stuff they didn't have to tell us. There was no legal requirement. The amateur administrator expects everyone to be friendly and lovely. The commercial reality is otherwise. The deal was the deal. What we had to do was get out of it."

Further investigation of the television landscape arrived through consultants of the solicited variety. Swinburne University lecturer Trevor Barr produced a report,

Future Directions for Australian Commercial Television and Cricket, in March, 1987, that pointed out how changes in ownership laws meant that the large networks—in cricket's case the Bond-owned Nine—were soon going to be in a position to charge higher fees to regional networks for sub-licensed programming:

> Whilst the Bond Corporation will produce arguments in favour of dramatic cost increases to them, the ACB must point out that under the policy of equalisation, all networks will be able to charge from 50-250 per cent increase of cost programs sold by the network to the regional operators. This revenue raiser for the networks did not exist when the ACB-PBL contract was negotiated in 1979. Equalisation, where much of regional television throughout Australia will get three commercial television channels, has increased the reach for Australian cricket telecasts, but has also increased the value of the ACB product to the network.

Another, bigger name brought into the ACB consulting fold was Harold Mitchell, the television advertising impresario who had provided, by his own estimation, "half of the advertisers for his World Series Cricket coverage on the Nine Network". Mitchell thus had significant knowledge of the amount of advertising revenue generated by cricket, and duly advised the Board in March, 1987 that annual returns from telecasts of ACB matches raked in "a probable revenue of $15 million plus", while also echoing Barr's reference to regional operators.

In his report to the Board, Mitchell went on: "Cricket

is invaluable to a network on building revenue in difficult times and gaining ratings against a wide cross-section of viewers. A network would rather have cricket than see its opposition with it, though the Seven Network has problems in this regard because of its current commitment to tennis. Television stations have new owners and operators whose problems are best understood by the Board rather than adopting a bullying or auction tactic. Firm diplomacy will win the day. The networks have a tough financial outlook (although this could improve over time). A practical approach which is flexible by the Board that recognises this outlook could ultimately be more rewarding."

Richards had worked tirelessly alongside Lynton Taylor for most of the previous seven years, but chairman Gray sought and received a more direct role in negotiations for 1987. "It was a normal commercial negotiation," Gray says. The Bond-era PBL's first offer, tabled in May, was a substantial improvement promising $2.5 million a year, indexed at five per cent annually, while reducing PBL's share of gate and sponsorship from half to a third. Around the same time, another major party showed interest in taking up the PBL role—US promoter Mark McCormack's IMG, widely known for its global sale of broadcast rights for tennis and golf. On the other side of the fence, Fitzmaurice and PBL had to contend with the ABC's withdrawal from the deal where the national broadcaster paid $1 million a season to broadcast cricket to regional areas that Nine could not access. The balance of power was perceptibly shifting.

As talks intensified across the middle of the year, Gray found himself dealing one-on-one in Melbourne with Fitzmaurice in the Collins Street boardroom of Gray Johnson. The ACB's September, 1987 bid for $4.75 million annually, indexed at ten per cent over five years while capping PBL's share of gate and sponsorship at 30 per cent less costs, was baulked at by Fitzmaurice, Jones and Nine's chief executive Sam Chisholm. "A lot of it had been carried out by management, but with the impasse I got more involved," Gray said. "Jim Fitzmaurice came and it was just the two of us to try to make a deal. We weren't going to get there, they were being very adamant, and I do remember saying—and it shows how money has changed—'Give us $200,000 extra to go into a cricket foundation for young cricketers', and Jim left the room, got on the phone and they agreed to that."

That $200,000 was tipped in on top of a compromise deal worth $15 million to Australian cricket over five years—as much a cause for celebration in the ACB Boardroom as the sight of Allan Border's young team winning the World Cup in India in early November, even if Nine's Sydney and Melbourne stations preferred to show the Dudley Moore and Nastassja Kinski rom-com *Unfaithfully Yours*, rather than the second innings of the final. Merriman observed: "I was critical of Malcolm's criticism of Parish and Steele, the Parish-Bradman deal.

But he [Malcolm] took the bit between his teeth and said, 'It's not good enough', so he renegotiated very strongly, which balanced out OK. You weren't dealing with the same people, and Malcom took advantage of that—there was an opportunity to do it. When Kerry came back in... 'Shit, what's this?' But it's business."

Business was helped by that World Cup triumph over England at Eden Gardens, but it was followed by the strongest home summer showing by an Australian team since 1984's series win over Pakistan. At the end of a tense and television-friendly finish to the 1987 Boxing Day Test—Mike Whitney and Craig McDermott holding out New Zealand's Richard Hadlee and Danny Morrison in the closing overs for a draw—Australia won its first Test series against anyone, anywhere, since the retirements of Greg Chappell, Dennis Lillee and Rod Marsh in 1984. Border's team also went on to win the World Series Cup tri-series (against New Zealand and Sri Lanka), beating New Zealand 2-0 in the finals.

Fitzmaurice was more than content with the deal's terms—and the evolution of Nine's television coverage over the following three years showed a good deal of commitment on its part to keep the game growing. Although many of the WSC innovations of Nine's inventive producer David Hill were lauded, his departure for London and then a wildly successful career in American broadcasting left Fitzmaurice and Nine's director Brian Morelli to introduce numerous next-generation improvements. These included adding player names on uniforms (1988-89) and creating stump-cam (1989-90), while the use of graphics and statistics continued to improve.

"I was given a very free hand. It was basically, 'That's your area, get on with it'," Fitzmaurice says. "Warren (Jones) and I would talk from time to time about it, and Warren would get comments from an ACB Board member and say, 'I'm very pleased to hear that things are going nicely and we seem to have a good relationship', that sort of thing."

"Hilly (David Hill) had a huge influence on the way Nine developed with sport. But I think in terms of the innovation they brought to the coverage, the guy behind it all who was really the innovator, and the bloke who always remained fairly quiet, was the director Brian Morelli. He was outstanding and brought a lot of innovation to Nine."

These TV innovations were arriving at a time when Bradman had finally departed from his last formal role in the game, retiring from the SACA's ground and finance committee in 1986. In late 1984, he had been invited by Merriman to address the Australian team meeting ahead of the side's Adelaide Test encounter with the West Indies. After Bradman had accepted but before the team arrived, Kim Hughes had resigned as captain, leaving Allan Border to introduce his new team at the start of what would become a near-decade in charge. Border has recalled that he muddled through his first address, before taking his seat and listening to Bradman compare the challenge presented by Clive Lloyd's pace quartet and the Bodyline attack of England in 1932-33. "He acknowledged the difficulty of facing the West Indies—they weren't bowling directly at the body, but their pace was more relentless," Border wrote in his autobiography, *Beyond Ten Thousand*. "He offered encouragement only, which I thought was fair enough."

Several public appearances by Bradman were notable. He looked on impassively at the opening of Adelaide Oval's Clarrie Grimmett Gate in December, 1988, as his old antagonist Bill O'Reilly held forth on the Australian selection panel of 1938—of which Bradman was a member—ignoring Clarrie Grimmett's low-slung wrist spin for that year's Ashes tour. Bradman spoke at the opening of the Sir Donald Bradman Stand at the Adelaide Oval, ahead of the 1990 Test match against Pakistan, noting of SACA's decision to name it after him: "As I have never been one to dispute the umpire's decision, I accept that with pleasure".

At an earlier function, to mark his 80th birthday, in August, 1988, Bradman spoke about cricket's drive towards a more commercial and professional mode:

"I believe in sports people being properly rewarded for their services, but in many instances I fear there is a great danger in the dollar being such a dominant factor that it erodes the underlying integrity and purpose of sport. I still think that it is important for people to be dedicated, and to love what they are doing, as distinct from the rewards.

To give of their best, the players have to have an inner commitment."

But away from the public eye, Bradman maintained a level of anonymous influence summed up by Gray and Merriman. Upon becoming chairman, in October 1986, Gray travelled to Adelaide to meet Bradman for a cup of tea in the foyer of the Hilton Hotel, while he later failed in a request to have Bradman visit the Australian dressing room during the 1988 Bicentenary Test in Sydney. "When I became chairman I arranged to go to Adelaide because of who he was, just to talk to him," Gray recalls. "So we met for afternoon tea, and that was typical. We didn't go to the pub to have a beer. We had a pleasant but fairly formal talk about what his attitude was to things like the PBL deal and administration. I remember being in Sydney around the Bicentenary Test in 1988, and the players wanted to see him, so I asked him would he come down to the dressing room and see them and he was quite pre-emptory: 'Certainly not. I don't go to the dressing room'. He had certain rules about what he did and didn't do. As far as I was concerned, any relationship with him was fairly formal."

Less formal was the process by which Bradman became involved in another debate during Gray's chairmanship, in 1988-89, over the question of the ACB funding model for the states and, by extension, their voting rights. The system of dividing certain pools of revenue in line with the number of votes at the Board table—New South Wales,

Victoria and South Australia 3/14ths each, Western Australia and Queensland 2/14ths and Tasmania 1/14th—was under strain, and a move towards equalisation did eventually result in all states but Tasmania receiving equal cuts. However it was a parallel discussion, introduced by Western Australia, about changing voting rights, that included Bradman's direct involvement.

Guided by Gray, the former chairman Bob Parish had travelled to each state to discuss a change of financial structure. Merriman can recall meeting with South Australia's third director, Jim Grose, and hearing, to his astonishment, that SA was contemplating a move to each state having two directors, giving up one of their own in the process. "I actually had breakfast with him one day and said, 'What the hell are you doing? You're voting yourself out of the board', and it was, 'Oh no, we've got this view', and I couldn't convince him otherwise," Merriman says. "But Parish got Bradman to have a look at it, and Bradman wrote a paper that I saw, all the reasons why it [SA's proposal] was wrong. It was sensational stuff.

"His primary reason for opposing it was basically foundation membership. With foundation membership [Victoria, New South Wales and South Australia], we've carried the other Associations. We brought Western Australia in, we brought these other states in. It was historical, and based on factual arrangements made at the time. It basically was a history to justify the fact that where we were going [in terms of Broad structure] was right, rather than changing. It'd be interesting if he was still around what he'd think of today's structure [of nine independent directors], he'd probably agree with it. But bearing in mind he was very much an Association person, very much SACA."

Perhaps it was this affinity with SACA that had Bradman making a rare visit to the dressing rooms during the fifth Test between Australia and the West Indies at Adelaide Oval in February, 1989. It was the day of a 114-run stand for the ninth wicket between Dean Jones and Merv Hughes. As Mike Whitney later recalled to the Seven Network, this resulted in an exchange between Bradman and the West Indian fast bowler Patrick Patterson that both surprised and delighted all of Australia's players. "Viv [Richards] is introducing Sir Donald Bradman to the team," Whitney said. "He gets to Patrick Patterson; he was six-foot-five, and cut, and he's sitting there, just in the jock strap. And Patrick stands up, like a shadow's gone over Sir Donald, this guy was that big. And he said, 'Very pleased to meet you Sir Donald Bradman, but I would be thinking if you were playing today that I could bowl you out'. No-one had ever heard Sir Donald swear or get angry. People will tell you he never even said 'bloody'. But after that statement he looked back up at Patrick Patterson and he went, 'I don't know about that sonny, you couldn't getting effing Merv Hughes out today'. We all just went, 'He's human!'."

13

'I've just sacked Lynton Taylor'

At 7.30am on 30 July, 1990, Kerry Packer strode imperiously into Nine's Willoughby headquarters to retake control of the network. In the hours that followed he began a cost-cutting regime with flourish, famously declaring that no more alcohol was to be imbibed on the network's premises, and limiting executive lunches to precisely one hour's duration. It was in this climate that the chief executive Sam Chisholm took his leave of the company to join Rupert Murdoch's BSkyB in the UK. Chisholm was soon followed to London by Jim Fitzmaurice. "I had proposals before me," Fitzmaurice says, "and I had to decide whether I wanted to stay on under the new old regime, or would I take these opportunities and so I decided it was time to move, and I went to London."

At Packer's side was Lynton Taylor, the ACB's old antagonist, but also Packer's son James, who would take a close interest in discussions with the ACB over the next period of rights, to begin in 1994.

Changes were also afoot at the ACB. David Richards, who'd served as CEO since 1980, had begun to look further afield, and would ultimately move to the ICC, in 1993. During this time, Richards made sure that his eventual successor Graham Halbish was left in no doubt about the priority for the next deal: "I told Graham that when the time came for a new television rights deal to be struck, we should be firm in insisting that the television and marketing arrangements should be separated, with a television agreement the priority and with marketing being brought in-house. I also told Lynton Taylor that he would be dealing with Graham, not with me, as I would be moving to the ICC in London."

The ACB's successful operational, sponsorship and marketing effort at the 1992 World Cup—held in Australia and New Zealand—also contributed to an eagerness to change the parameters of the deal. Earlier concerns about needing PBL's salesmanship had faded, helped by the re-appearance of none other than Fitzmaurice, who, alongside the New Zealand entrepreneur Michael Watt at the broadcast rights packaging firm CSI, was doing for cricket, football and rugby what IMG had done for the professional tennis and golf tours over the preceding decade. CSI had worked with the ACB selling the rights to the World Cup.

Malcolm Gray, who after finishing as ACB chairman in 1989 had taken the role of World Cup chairman, danced something of a jig with Richards when the receipts came back for a tournament in which Allan Border's team had failed to qualify for the semi-finals despite heavy favouritism. Hoping merely to break even, the tournament made a surplus of $5 million. India had yet to emerge as a major television buyer, and the sale of UK rights to Sky Sports was the largest part of the deal.

"A complicating factor with your international deals with the World Cup in your other major markets was the time zone didn't work too well," Fitzmaurice says. "But we were generally pretty satisfied with the deals we did. The market wasn't too bad. There was a reasonable amount of interest. Pay television has made a big difference, but in those days you were looking at pretty restricted markets. Your biggest market is going to be the UK and then beyond that the deals are not great. This was in the days before India really became a major player, and they only became one because of the influence of Star TV, which also caused the traditional broadcasters to rethink the way they approached things—you couldn't buy something for nothing anymore."

When Alan Crompton, who had taken over from Col

Egar as ACB chair in 1992, met Taylor to express cricket's desire to run its own marketing through the next rights deadline, Taylor offered him a thinly veiled threat. The minutes of the next Board meeting stated: "Mr Taylor observed that Nine/PBLM were regarded as one entity re cricket and that if the ACB did not accept that, then Nine would not carry ACB cricket in future, but it would carry cricket." Yet subsequent events showed Packer had no desire for another breakaway.

Richards was aware of Taylor's attitude, and counselled Halbish to be firm. "The message that was very clearly delivered was that the nexus between a marketing agreement and a television agreement was going to be broken," Richards says. "Lynton wasn't at all happy about that, because I think he was trying to perpetuate the deal that had been done back in 1979. But that's not the way it panned out. That's the basis on which Australian cricket is organised these days—has been for a very long time and the way it should be done."

This is not to say that Taylor observed the change in ACB chief executives without trying to influence events. What he found, however, was that the Board was nowhere near as ready to read his views as gospel, as they once had been. This was summed up by an evening meeting with Bob Merriman. "The night before Graham was appointed [in 1993], Lynton Taylor rang me and asked me to go to dinner with him," Merriman says. "Lynton said to me that as far as he was concerned Graham should not be

CEO. I said, 'Lynton I'm not being lobbied by you, I know which way I'm going to vote, I'm going to want us to go out to the market without disqualifying Graham'. He said, 'That's fair enough', but Lynton was absolutely opposed."

Early negotiations were far from promising. As recalled by Halbish in his memoir, *Run Out*[19], Taylor's early offer was for a financial upside far less substantial than that just offered by the World Cup: "The Nine Network was paying the ACB $2 million a year, and now it would be extremely generous and increase it to $3 million. I said 'bullshit' to that." Changes to the PBL deal in Taylor's absence during the Bond years at Nine had not only included an increase in the ACB's annual share of the game's revenue, but also an adjustment to account for fees payable to the Board for the rights to overseas tours.

With the help of Fitzmaurice, consulting to the ACB for CSI, Halbish confirmed that apart from its annual revenue-sharing arrangement, Nine/PBL owed the ACB around $3 million in unpaid rights fees for overseas tours. After getting little response from Taylor, Crompton and Halbish confronted Kerry Packer at Park Street, after they had been invited by David Leckie, who had taken over as managing director from Chisholm. As Crompton was quoted in *Inside Story*: "Within five minutes he'd come back and told us, 'Tear up that invoice. We'll send you a credit note for the same sum. And by the way, I've just sacked Lynton Taylor'." When Packer said he would take

19 *Run Out*, Graham Halbish (Lothian, 2003)

over talks personally, Halbish pushed back by saying he was already making progress with Leckie. Impressed, Packer gave gruff approval.

"When Kerry repurchased Nine in 1990, I started preparing the negotiations for the renewal," Taylor says. "It was during that period that James started to get involved. He had this view that Kerry and I had been too hard on the Board and should become friends with them, not antagonistic in terms of negotiation. So, he (James) basically took over the negotiations [with Leckie], and that's when things started to slip away. Crompton and Halbish started talking to James about the fact I was too tough, they didn't like negotiating with me. That was the end as far as I was concerned."

The fruit of their talks was a new deal announced to the Board in March, 1994. It lifted the ACB into the sort of comfortable financial position it has enjoyed ever since. The PBL tie was severed, and Nine agreed to pay a rights fee worth $55 million over five years, while also pledging advertising support for the game. Finally, cricket would get a share of the game's revenue commensurate with its value. Finally, cricket would direct its own path in terms of how it sold and programmed itself. Finally, Australia's best players would be paid something comparable to the money available to top athletes in other national sports. Cricket had not moved on from Nine, but it had moved ahead.

For some, like the just-retired Border, and Dean Jones, the new deal arrived too late; Border's final contract with the ACB for 1993-94 was worth a mere $90,000. For others, like Shane Warne, Mark Taylor and the Waugh twins, money would no longer be a source of worry. Within three years, the Australian Cricketers Association was founded, and after initial ructions in 1997-98, the first players' Memorandum of Understanding (MOU) was signed off to grant a fixed share of the game's revenue, and professional wages, to state players. The ACB became Cricket Australia, the modest Academy in Adelaide evolved into the monolithic National Cricket Centre in Brisbane, and the top Test players became millionaires.

Lynton Taylor reflects, ruefully, that this was also the deal that definitively shifted the balance of power away from Packer and Nine towards the ACB and its administrators. "That's when they started giving their rights away," he says. "Kerry was still alive, but he wasn't 100 per cent at the company. That was the first contract without my negotiations. The next round was David Leckie and James and basically they gave everything up in that next round of negotiations. They gave up their rights to World Series Cricket footage, they gave everything away that had been won back in 1979. Since then they've just been paying more and more and more and getting nothing back."

Given the circumstances in which Taylor was pushed, the last tour covered by Nine under the auspices of the Packer-Bradman "peace treaty" was somewhat ironic—the first official tour of South Africa since the end of apartheid. In the preceding few years a unique situation had evolved, where major tours such as trips to England (1985, 1989, 1993), the West Indies (1991) and South Africa (1994) were beamed into Australian homes on Nine. Fittingly, the last match of the '94 tour was a floodlit limited overs match at Bloemfontein, in which Border's team held their nerve to secure a narrow victory defending a modest target—a recurring and much-enjoyed scenario for Australian cricket watchers over the preceding 10 years. But by the time the national team, now led by Mark Taylor, travelled to the West Indies in 1995, overseas broadcast rights were no longer of interest to Nine or Packer: the nascent pay-television provider Galaxy won the rights, before a public outcry ended with them being on-sold to Ten. It was all part of a change that, as Fitzmaurice recounts, created a second pot of gold for cricket Boards across the globe:

"The really big thing that Australian cricket benefited from internationally, in terms of revenue—and television provides the big share of the revenue—was pay television. Pay-television utterly changed the face of sports negotiations throughout the world. The first big presence was Sky in London, and Sam [Chisholm] was running that, and Sam and I worked together for a number of years. Working with him, I was very quickly realising that pay-television was going to become a big buyer of sport throughout the world.

"The point about that was not only what pay-TV was

paying, but pay-television was providing competition. Worldwide, generally what it did was create competition, and big competition. In markets where there was no alternative buyer, you either deal with a state broadcaster or you don't deal. In those cases, suddenly there was someone on the block who was quite serious about it. That dramatically increased the sort of numbers that started to be paid for sport, and it hasn't gone away. That had a massive flow-on effect for all cricket boards and all sporting bodies. You simply wouldn't have the sort of money you see going around these days, you wouldn't be anywhere near it without those changes."

In 1995 Fitzmaurice was involved in the selling of 10-year global rights for world rugby to Rupert Murdoch's News Corporation for a fee worth US$555 million. And by 2000, Gray, as ICC president, found himself signing on the dotted line for a figure of similar magnitude for cricket. "We made $5 million for the 1992 World Cup and we thought we were kings of commerce," he says, laughing. "Whereas in 2000, I remember flying to Monaco as ICC chairman to sign a contract for $500 million for five years of World Cups and other competitions. Less than 10 years before we were pretty happy we'd got $5 million!"

Either way, the ACB's handling of the end of the peace treaty certainly left its mark on Packer. After returning to Melbourne from the meeting that ended Lynton Taylor's years in cricket, Halbish received a call from Leckie. "Kerry wanted to let you know," Leckie said, as recalled by Halbish in *Run Out*, "that he thinks Australian cricket has finally grown some balls."

In June 1994, Tim Caldwell, who had played an integral part in that fateful 1979 meeting between Bradman and Packer, died. His funeral in Orange brought with it a certain sense of closure for many. The new landscape was being redrawn by the day, from the drafting of a new ACB logo and the formulation of the Board's first non-PBL advertising and marketing campaigns, to the early planning of a new captain in Mark Taylor, who carried a strong sense of cricket's newfound independence.

Parish, Packer, Bradman and Taylor had few regrets about the way the previous 15 years had unfolded. As Parish told *The Sydney Morning Herald* at the time of Caldwell's funeral: "You've got to realise we were losing a lot of money in Australia. Certain Associations were really, really in financial difficulties. The pressure from other countries was great, too. I think you would have seen World Series Cricket start up all over the world. Packer wasn't going to walk away from it even though it was costing him a lot of money. But he could afford it. We couldn't. It was time for Australia to arrive at a solution, and it was because of the Tim Caldwells and the Bradmans that we arrived at a solution. Packer was right. And I think we were very fortunate to have people like Caldwell and Bradman during those two difficult years. Tim had an ability to get to the bottom of things without fuss and without a lot of bravado. He was a very solid citizen."

While Caldwell's legacy was to be appreciated only by a small circle of cricket administrators, Bradman's was in the process of being preserved for all time. His museum at Bowral was under construction, with uncertain funding flows to pay for it all—a situation that was to reunite him, in a sense, with Packer. During the winter of 1994, Packer and Tony Greig stepped in with an idea: a televised fundraising match between a Bradman XI and a World XI, staged under lights at the SCG.

Greig threw himself into the project, assembling a collection of cricket luminaries: Brian Lara, Sunil Gavaskar, Graeme Pollock, Barry Richards, Michael Holding, Joel Garner, Abdul Qadir, Dennis Lillee, Greg Chappell, Jeff Thomson, Doug Walters and David Hookes were among the players. There were also a host of novelties about the day, from the players being kitted out in baseball uniforms and the use of an experimental multi-coloured ball, to individual batsmen and bowlers being mic'd up. The Bradman-Packer association, revived over the course of this match, would evolve into Ray Martin's interview with Bradman and the $1 million telethon a little over a year later.

Bradman did not attend the game, but had a say in its organisation: he was particularly eager for Lara to play. We can only guess his reaction when the new holder of the game's two major batting world records was dismissed by Australian women's team all-rounder Zoe Goss, but he was satisfied by a day in which 17,456 spectators turned up to the SCG and handed over gate takings worth $278,000. The ground was provided free of charge, while PBL/Nine had agreed to pay for flights and accommodation for all players. Television advertising revenue, in keeping with the most contentious clause of the peace treaty, stayed with Nine.

Some remarked at the time how ironic it was that the most Packer/PBL-styled event of the entire summer was a venture designed to venerate Sir Donald Bradman. Had they known the story behind it, the arrangement would not have seemed so surprising. Bradman had once looked after Packer. Fifteen years later, Packer returned the favour.

14

Still Influential

I f the end of the ACB-PBL deal broke the bond that had lasted since Packer flew to Adelaide to meet Bradman in February 1979, it did not mean that Australia's richest man and his acolytes ceased to wield any influence over Australian cricket. In fact, given the loss of contractual power over the game and the ACB's decisions around its scheduling and promotion, what emerged instead was a tendency to interject with opinions as readily, if not more so, than during the 1979-87 and 1990-94 periods, either side of Alan Bond's brief ownership of Nine and PBL.

Mark Taylor was among the first to be made aware of this, after making plain his displeasure about the Australia A concept—a side comprised of the significant cohort of brilliant players, young and old, who couldn't break into the strong Australian side—devised by the ACB in 1994 to pad out a World Series Cup competition that featured a mediocre England side and a fledgling Zimbabwe. Although it was not his idea, Packer told some lieutenants that he wished he'd thought of it, until Taylor expressed his displeasure with the concept when the senior team was booed at Adelaide Oval while completing a narrow win over the second-string side, which was, by then, attracting a cult following as the underdog. Taylor said at the time: "I didn't enjoy the game. I don't enjoy playing against my teammates. To me it was like a trial game and I'm never at my best in trials."

Looking back now, Taylor says it was the first time he was made aware of a larger presence looming over the game than anyone he had dealt with to that point. "I knew that Kerry was very keen on the Australia A concept because we had Zimbabwe and England here, and I didn't like the idea as Australian captain," Taylor says. "I'd said something in the media about not enjoying playing against my fellow countrymen, and it got back to me that Kerry wasn't very happy with me for saying that, because he honestly wanted to see contests, and more games."

The prism offered by Taylor is one of the best through which to observe events of the years that followed. Packer continued to wield his financial might, while Bradman's profile re-grew and evolved to that of the revered elder statesman of a game that, in Australia at least, was enjoying considerable rejuvenation behind the success of Taylor's team. Helped by the television deal struck in 1994, and others quickly building up in the pay television sphere, the best Australian players were earning the sort of money they had long envied when considering the fortunes of players in other sports. This despite the fact that, until the inception of the Australian Cricketers Association in 1997, Taylor would be the only players' representative entitled to an audience with the Board.

"I noticed that when I took over the captaincy in 1994, that I was still going as the player representative to sit in front of the Board," Taylor says. "I can recall doing that two or three times, where the Board invited me in and you'd walk into the Boardroom. You can imagine how daunting that was, as a captain, to confront the Board— all 14 of them, plus the CEO and a few others. You're sitting around a massive table and you're the lone voice of the players. It was certainly a daunting experience."

The financial conservatism on the Board deviated little from Bradman's well-entrenched attitude. The treasurer during this period remained the South Australian Des Rundle, after whose family Adelaide's central mall was named. Malcolm Gray recalls Rundle's running of the Board's finances as treasurer from 1985 to 1998: "He did the job as treasurer like an accountant would with keeping the petty cash balanced, as opposed to strategy or position. Apart from that he was virtually a delegate from South

Australia, as opposed to being an independent ACB director."

For Merriman, power on the Board was shifting towards the Tasmanian Denis Rogers, who emerged as Crompton's successor in late 1995 and would go on to hold the post until 2001, but he could see in Rundle the heavy influence of Bradman. "ACB administration couldn't spend a dollar without Des's approval," Merriman says. "Very strong Bradman influence there, and Des and Bradman were very close. If you ask me the question about Bradman's influence after (the peace deal), it came through Rundle. Colin Egar on the playing conditions and umpiring, but Rundle certainly on the money; 'Make sure the state Association gets a lot of money, full stop'. That was where Bradman's influence was after 1980, because Des came onto the Board as soon as Bradman retired. His view about player payments was a lot different from mine and a lot different from others, but he was a finance man who managed the dollars very carefully."

One man whose eventual demise related to careful financial management—one key problem among many others, including differences of personality and process with Rogers—was Graham Halbish. Within a couple of years of playing his key role in ending the PBL axis, Halbish's venture into the short-form and short-lived "Super 8s" concept (eight players per side, 14-over matches) with CSI and News Corporation, would contribute to Rogers summoning the forces of the Board to dismiss him, acrimoniously, in January, 1997. "The Super 8s issue was a catalyst at the finish," Merriman recalls. "There was enough going on—the players issue was starting to bubble, Denis had had a number of experiences of Graham not consulting with him on key issues, and Graham doing things outside his authority.

"We'd been to play Super 8s in Malaysia [in 1996], but Denis was starting to get worried about it before that. So Denis sent me to Malaysia [in 1997] as the manager of the side, and Richard Watson was up there running it—a good operator caught in between Denis and Graham. A terrible squeeze. I went up there, looked at it, watched it, came back and said, 'This is not going to work'. It was costing us too much money. So I actually moved at a meeting that we were not to spend another cent on it, until we finalised the Malaysian exercise, until we get a projection about what we should be looking at, what it might be worth broadcasting-wise—all aspects.

"So the Board's position was that Graham was not to spend another penny ... but he went off overseas again selling Super 8s, and didn't say boo to us. Graham didn't tell anyone he was going to Japan or anything, and just gave us a bloody report to say what had happened. He had no authority to do A, B, C or D and that's what sparked Denis off." Halbish maintained in his account of events that he did nothing more than embark upon longer term planning for Super 8s that the Board was free to shelve if and when it saw fit. At the same time he embarked upon meetings with News Corporation about longer-term pay TV rights for the short format—talks that were cut short when he was summarily dismissed in January, 1997.

Halbish's sacking took place in the midst of Taylor's infamous run of outs in the first half of 1997, but by the time an Edgbaston hundred had shored up his captaincy, the "players issue" was starting to do a lot more than bubble. Before the end of the '97 Ashes tour, conservative money management, combined with the players' gathering prominence, and knowledge of the Board's growing coffers, led to the forming of the Australian Cricketers Association in 1997 and the pay dispute that followed it. The Board's most critical contribution to the dispute was to publicise the earnings of the leading players: a mere three years after Border's $90,000 final contract, Taylor, Steve Waugh, Glenn McGrath, Shane Warne and Ian Healy were all earning in the region of $440,000 each.

The players' valid point of dispute, however, was that their overall share of the burgeoning revenue was too low, and the base too narrow, with domestic cricketers still only semi-professional, with day jobs to balance their training and playing commitments. As Taylor remembers, the strengthening of the team and, as a consequence, its more settled nature, created a far better environment for the players to question the pay model than was the case during the uncertainty of the 1980s. "We were improving all the time and also that group of players—the Waughs, the Healys, myself, Shane Warne, Glenn McGrath—all of a sudden we had a far more senior group and we became more aware during that time of other things in the game," he says. "When you first start out you just want to bat, bowl and field and stay in the team. But obviously as time goes on and you become a senior player, you start to hear or read things."

While numerous inflammatory figures, including a gamekeeper-turned-poacher in Halbish, were now working for the players, and the ambitious management figure of James Erskine pushed the dispute towards possible strike action in limited overs games in late 1997, Packer privately encouraged Taylor and other senior players to keep such action as a last resort. He did so via Nine's then head of sport Gary Burns, who dined with Taylor and Warne during the Perth Test against New Zealand a matter of weeks before the one-day games that would have been subject to a work stoppage. For the ACB, the dispute's resolution meant that the end of one revenue-sharing arrangement with PBL was replaced with another, this time with the players. In Merriman's mind, the difficulty in getting Board agreement for the concept could still be traced back to financial scars, both real and imagined, from WSC.

"Because of the additional money that became available, there was a significant move in player payments, but mainly only for the top fifteen. That's what probably led us to the 1997 problem," he says. "Clearly before that, and I go back to Bob Parish, who'd say, 'We'll pay what we can afford', and nobody would believe that was all we could afford. But Parish's 'pay what we can afford' was after we looked after grassroots, not just the players. The players argued, 'We generate the money, so we should get the bigger share'. Those were the two different viewpoints.

"Cricket administration had the view that we'll pay the players but we've got to look after whoever was playing the game, and that was to make sure the state associations stayed alive. Parish got that out of the fright that everybody got from the WSC experience—from 1977 to 1979, when cricket wasn't making any money. That was always a firm idea for him, and that followed with Alan Crompton too, because he had experienced that same pain, and also Des Rundle."

As the dispute settled down in 1998, Halbish's replacement, Malcolm Speed, found himself negotiating the next TV deal largely with James Packer. "A not infrequent event," Speed wrote in his autobiography, "was to agree on several points in the current draft and then find at the next meeting that a point that had been agreed two or three meetings before had been changed back to its original form. We needed to be on our toes." But at the time agreement was finally reached—this time for a deal lasting from 1999 until 2005, and rising in value from $25 million to $30 million a season over the course of the contract, and $195 million in total—James Packer's relief was more than apparent to Speed.

This desire to secure cricket itself, and much of the

talent within it, was to be experienced by Mark Taylor, too. "I was approached by James Packer to sign up with Nine, probably 18 months out from the end of my career, very much along the lines of a loyalty deal," he says. "In hindsight it was probably twofold looking back. One to keep me not looking elsewhere to maybe ply my trade if there were other opportunities, but secondly they were looking even than at the commentary side of the game. Because as soon as I was finished, I did have a catchup with Kerry about joining Nine as a commentator.

"The first time was at a place called Beppi's in Sydney, a restaurant in Stanley Street in East Sydney. That was before I actually signed up. Part of the signing up was having lunch with Kerry and we chatted. He didn't grill you, but chatted away about cricket, golf, horse racing. He loved his sport. I think after about a two- or three-hour lunch, Kerry got up and said, 'Well Mark, nice to catch up and maybe we can do something going forward,' and walked out, and that was it. I didn't know if I had a job at the end of that or not. That was left to Gary Burns, who was the head of sport at the time. It was probably a month or two after that I signed up as a commentator for Nine."

The abiding admiration for sportsmen that had flavoured Packer's dealings with Bradman in 1979 was still very evident to Taylor, as shown by the pride with which Packer told the story of working assiduously to be both fit and skilled enough to hold his own alongside Greg Norman at the 1992 Pebble Beach Pro-Am.

"He apparently worked his butt off for a year and a half or something like that," Taylor says. "Plenty of golf lessons and rounds to get himself down to a handicap of seven, just so he could play in this Pro-Am with Norman. He and Greg went ahead and won it, and that would've been one of his sporting highlights, for sure. To win that, and to get down to such a low handicap." Norman himself remarked to the journalist Peter Stone in the *Sydney Morning Herald* of one conversation with Packer in which the billionaire ruminated on a very specialised form of poverty:

"Greg, you have something I'll never have."

"What do you mean?" replied Norman.

"You are No.1 in the world, and I'll never be No.1."

Taylor's retirement as a player, in 1999, was a source of a little less consternation than it might have been without his talks with the Packers. With uncanny timing, Taylor was to find favour with Bradman, through a famous innings and an equally famous decision at the end of it. Upon his return home from declaring on 334 not out against Pakistan at Peshawar in 1998, Taylor received the following letter from Bradman: "Might I take this opportunity of congratulating you on your wonderful batting performance overseas during which you equalled my 334. It was extremely generous of you to declare when our scores were level—a most sportsmanlike act—when you could have so easily gone on to take the record for yourself. Your recognition of the interests of the team will never be forgotten."

This correspondence was accompanied by an invitation to meet with Bradman at his home, still 2 Holden Street. As vivid as anything was the fact that in the course of speaking with Bradman, Taylor reckoned with the sharp and inquiring mind of a long-time ACB director, rather than that of the ageing former batsman and captain he had expected. "I must admit I went there thinking it would be a reasonably quick conversation based on me making 334, the same score as he, but we hardly even talked about that," Taylor says. "He was talking about match-fixing that came out of Pakistan a couple of years earlier, which unfortunately had become part of the game. He was up on all the recent issues. He wanted to know about Warney's shoulder and all that sort of stuff.

"He certainly had his finger on the pulse of the news of the game at the time. It wasn't just about who was winning and who was losing, it was the stuff off the field. I do recall talking about the match-fixing stuff that came out of Pakistan a couple of years earlier, so he certainly wanted to know all about that. Still very sharp, very keen on the game, but also very private. He didn't want to go to Adelaide Oval and have it, he wanted to be in a private place where we could have a chat, say what he wanted to say, and not be drawn into the public."

When Bradman died, in February 2001, the Indian and Australian teams stood for a minute's silence in Mumbai before the start of a Test series played in the kind of attacking, dramatic spirit Bradman had always pushed for. Less often remembered is that for the memorial service broadcast live around Australia by the ABC from St Peter's Cathedral in Adelaide, the Bradman family expressed his wish that the coverage be hosted by Packer's man, Ray Martin. On a day when every other request was granted, the ABC stood firm: commentary duties were instead taken on by Tony Squires, one of their own.

15

Packer's Last Stand

In the days before the final Test of the 2005 Ashes series in England, Bob Merriman was driving home from Melbourne to his Point Lonsdale home when the phone rang. Having served in all manner of roles in Australian cricket since the late 1970s, he had, since 2001, been the chairman of what was now known as Cricket Australia. Not many phone calls surprised him, but this one did: Kerry Packer was on the line.

"Get that fucking Hussey in the side, quick," Packer insisted.

"Kerry," Merriman retorted, "the selectors will pick the side."

"They can't pick a bloody club team, Martyn hasn't made a run!"

Startled by Packer's adamant approach, Merriman called his chief executive, James Sutherland.

"Please remind Trevor Hohns that he can pick any Australian, he doesn't have to pick from the 17."

"What do you mean?" Sutherland asked.

"Just let him know that."

Minutes pass, and Sutherland calls back with a response about the obvious player: "Bob, Mike Hussey's on a plane now, we can't get him in."

Hussey was in fact on his way from England to Pakistan for an Australia A tour, alongside the touring party's reserve wicketkeeper, Brad Haddin. But the fact that his unavailability was dictated less by opposition to Packer's request than by a previous engagement is as great a reminder as any of Packer's ability to influence events.

At that point Packer was only a few months away from his death on the first day of the 2005 Boxing Day Test, but his final year was among his most eventful so far as Australian cricket was concerned. Packer, alongside Nine's chief executive David Gyngell and opposite Merriman and Sutherland, had taken on one last television deal for cricket. It took place amid the emergence of Twenty20, and was underpinned by other market factors on which Packer had made his strong sentiments known to the game's Australtian custodians.

One such factor was an increasingly motley international schedule, as the bilateral commitments of full ICC nations (such as Australia) were opened up to the likes of

Zimbabwe and Bangladesh. These nations toured Australia for Tests in 2003 and 2004 respectively. Packer aired his views to Merriman, calling such series "wallpaper", and making a particular point about Matthew Hayden's world record score against Zimbabwe in October 2003, at the WACA Ground. "It was the Matthew Hayden 380 that he claimed had cost him $4 million," Merriman says. "The match was in the last week of the ratings period and all his good programs weren't on because of the three-hour time difference. And that week he went down the gurgler on ratings like you wouldn't believe, and he's out there trying to sell for the next year. I don't know how he made up the $4 million, but his ratings figures disappeared, because nobody was watching Australia versus Zimbabwe, even though Hayden was making 380."

Packer wanted to see more of England, India, South Africa and the West Indies, and he was also skeptical of Twenty20 (T20), the "next generation" form of the game that had been unveiled in England during the northern summer of 2003. T20's arrival has passed into history as a game-changing moment for cricket, but in its earliest days, there was as much doubt among broadcasters as existed among players. For just as Queensland's then captain Jimmy Maher stated the need to ensure everyone was aware that it wasn't "real cricket", in the first season of the Big Bash, so too had media buyers and sellers seen plenty of short-form ventures come and go.

Super 8s and Martin Crowe's Cricket Max (10 8-ball

overs per team of 13 players) were two, while the Hong Kong Sixes had not expanded beyond the location from which they took their name. And at a time when rivers of gold were still flowing into pay-TV networks for the game's conventional forms, many simply did not see the need, Jim Fitzmaurice among them. "T20 crept up on a lot of people, there was a certain amount of cynicism about it from the beginning, and no-one really expected that it would pull the sorts of audiences it did," he says. "Short-form sport has been around for quite a while, and it wasn't unusual every few months to have someone coming through the door telling you this was the new format which someone had invented for cricket, golf, rugby. Someone was always coming up with a pattern where they wanted to shorten the game and make it more exciting. And a lot of it didn't even get tried because you looked at the formula and said, 'That ain't going to work'."

When comparing it to the number of hours of programming—and advertising breaks—provided by Test matches and ODIs, Packer soon made clear his attitude: T20 played by Australia was of some interest, but domestic tournaments were of little use to him. By now established as a commentator and having recently joined the Board of what was now Cricket Australia, Mark Taylor discussed the format with Packer after Nine hosted the first broadcast of a T20 game in Australia, between the touring Pakistanis and Australia A in Adelaide, in January 2005. "I had a chat with Kerry not long after and asked him what he thought of T20. He wasn't a big fan because he considered the game too short and that there was not enough time to make money out of it. He said, 'Yes, there's probably a place for it, but it's not in the place of one-day cricket', and that was Kerry saying it's not a bad product, but I don't want it taking over my one-day cricket. That's the way I read it."

One-day cricket had not quite lost its lustre, certainly not in the form it took when CA and the Australian Cricketers Association rapidly organised a fundraising match in the wake of the Boxing Day Tsunami, to be held at the MCG in January, 2005. Towards the end of the night, Merriman accompanied Malcolm Speed, by then the ICC chief executive, to announce the amount of money raised by the occasion. As Speed spoke, a figure of $10.5 million turned, in a trice, to $14.5 million via "the Packer family". The punchline arrived later in summer. "A few weeks later we had lunch with Kerry. James Packer is there, [senior Nine executive] John Alexander's there, and James Sutherland and I. The first thing I said was, 'Kerry, on behalf of cricket and everybody, I'd like to thank the family for the $4 million', and he turns to James and says (sarcastically), 'How much did you put in James? No fucking money at all'. James just looked at him!"

There were more than a few power lunches around this time, and as many revelations. "One day we were talking a little bit about WSC," Merriman says. "I said, 'You're bloody lucky those lights in Sydney stood up—not as good as the lights in Melbourne you paid for', and James Packer says, 'You paid for those lights in Melbourne too!' And Kerry just says, 'Of course I fucking did'."

While technology was advancing, sport remained a highly reliable source of large audiences, even as other forms of television lost their former attractiveness. "People generally forecast that with the widespread development of other technologies and other methods of distribution, not necessarily through traditional television networks, that the value of sporting rights would gradually diminish because the audiences were going to get smaller and smaller," Fitzmaurice says. "In Australia the average audiences that networks now attract don't compare with what they were doing in the 1980s, and the trend is that gradually people and particularly young people look for other sources.

"They don't sit down at their television at a prescribed time determined by the broadcaster. That means that you don't get the big movie nights anymore, or mini-series, and you'd get really big audiences to them. All that's gone. However, live sport remains one of the final few products that free-to-air television can get hold of and still get the sorts of audiences they used to get in the 1980s. It's one of the few things that still attracts a mass audience. That's why you've got a change in the sort of television diet offered by traditional broadcasters."

It was in this climate that Nine and CA commenced negotiations for Packer's last cricket deal, to run from

2006 to 2013. The groundwork was done with agreement that its many detailed clauses would be worked through by Sutherland and Gyngell, while Merriman and Packer would meet later in the process to haggle over the dollars involved. In late 2004, Packer called Merriman to Melbourne's Crown Casino to express concern that the chief executives were taking too long sorting through the detail. "I didn't say it," Merriman recalls, "but it was obvious his health wasn't great." Among the many changes wrought by the deal was the move to live coverage against the gate in Melbourne and Sydney, irrespective of ticket sales. From the beginning of the PBL/ACB deal, only the last session of Tests, and the first two hours of ODIs, were shown live into the city of origin unless a match was sold out.

When the time came in early May, 2005, to conclude the deal with a final day's negotiation, Merriman got an unpleasant surprise. Packer did not want Nine to have to broadcast the Twenty20 Big Bash, a new, state-based tournament, that CA had scheduled for the following summer. "This T20 cricket is no fucking good," Packer declared. "When do I make a dollar? The batsmen change on the ground; there's no time; there's a small lunch break; there's no tea break; there's no drinks break. When do I make my fucking money?"

"Oh, so you don't want it," Merriman replied.

"No, no, 50-over cricket is the thing I want."

Suddenly worried by the scene unfolding, Merriman

called for a break. "So James [Sutherland] and I and Gyngell went out of the room and I said to James, 'Go and make a couple of calls to see if pay-TV want T20. See what you can do—the Shield final has got to be in it', and Fox got it," he says. "Even though we only got about $6 million for it, we got an opening for it. We were going to have no-one to telecast it, that was the biggest thing." This separate deal, pulled together quickly as Fox Sports also gained non-live highlights to international matches, meant that Merriman could return to dealing with Packer on more comfortable ground.

"That's off the table, you don't need to worry about that," Merriman told Packer about the Big Bash and the Shield final.

"What do you mean?"

"You don't need to worry about that. I give in."

The afternoon was now wearing on, and Packer eventually met the figure Merriman was seeking: $275 million over seven years. "The clock was up on the wall and I said to him, 'What time's that?' He said, 'What do you mean?' I said, 'What time's that?' And he said, 'It's five to five, what do you mean?' And I said, 'We've got a deal,' and shook his hand. He said, 'You're going to go out there, and you'll have grog, and you'll say how you did Kerry Packer'." But Packer had, in fact, wrested back one clause given up by James Packer when dealing with Speed in 1998: the requirement for Nine to underwrite at the end of the deal. "It was in the last bloody deal and I didn't like it," Packer told Merriman. "I was sick in hospital and bloody Denis Rogers put it over James'."

Merriman and Sutherland got a brief fright in the following weeks when Packer re-hired Lynton Taylor to work alongside Gyngell, who soon quit in frustration at being watched over in such a way. But the deal stood, and so too the split of domestic T20 away from Nine. The tournament remained a Fox Sports property when it was re-launched as the Big Bash League in 2011, and then became critical extra ballast for the first post-Packer deal in 2013. Nine was pushed to a still higher figure by the added interest of Ten, which failed to claim the whole cricket package but still walked away with the BBL for $20 million a season. Together, the new agreement was worth $590 million to CA over five summers.

"We used to always do the international T20 matches but a lot of that domestic stuff Nine didn't pick up," Mark Taylor says. "You can say that's a mistake, but as Kerry would've pointed out if he was around, it's not just about the cricket, it's also about the business. Whether he would've made enough money out of it, I don't know. I wasn't privy enough to what was going on behind the scenes then. It would've been interesting had Nine picked it up, even in 2013 when it went to Ten from Fox; if Nine had done the whole lot, where we would have landed today?"

Almost forty years after the first deal between Nine and the ACB, that landing resulted in the shift of cricket away from Packer's old network to the pay-television wing of Rupert Murdoch's News Corp, with free-to-air rights to Tests, BBL and WBBL on-sold to Kerry Stokes's Seven Network. In turn, Nine took over Seven's grip on the Australian Open tennis tournament. In April, 2018, Australian cricket's domestic TV rights deal topped the $1 billion mark for the first time, as Fitzmaurice's view of sport's broad-based attraction to television held true despite the Newlands ball-tampering scandal. For the first time, too, the women's game made up a substantial part of the deal, thanks largely to the persistent lobbying of CA's head of media rights, Stephanie Beltrame. The third major broadcasting deal of his 18 years as CA's chief executive was also James Sutherland's last.

Kerry Packer made a lasting impression on Sutherland. "He wanted Nine to own the big stuff, the really important stuff, and he was a great traditionalist when it came to international cricket," Sutherland says. "Nine was broadly suspicious of T20 cricket and state cricket. Even this year [2018], when we did the TV deal, Nine was very much about Test cricket. They wanted international cricket, but once they got the tennis they were still very much in the game around Test cricket, and had a really strong view and belief in its longevity and importance.

"No organisation has put more into cricket financially or promoted it more than the Nine Network, and Australian cricket should always be incredibly grateful for that. That's Kerry's legacy—World Series Cricket and then owning the rights when he was the principal of Nine. But beyond that, if you really love the game you should be positive about the game, and promote the game. Kerry was very strong on that, so much so that as folklore has it he'd ring the commentary box and have people talk the game up, to the extent he'd give them one warning and might not give them two."

"Sure there are things to be critical of, or things that may be different, but it just concerns me when some people get to the stage in life where, even though they proclaim to be genuine lovers of the game, all they can do is criticise. I think it's sad that it's come to that, and maybe they've just done one too many laps."

Former Nine commentator Mark Nicholas has chronicled his own phone call, received in the summer of 2004-05, after he had gone to some length describing how cold and dank it was in Hobart, how the crowd was rugged up and how the touring Pakistani team was trying as best it could to keep warm.

"Son, stop telling us how fucking cold it is in Hobart and how the fielders are wringing their hands and how people are wrapped in anoraks and having a shit time," Packer ordered. "The only people having a shit time are those of us at home who have to sit here fucking listening to you. And son, we're a commercial network. We sell the game. It's not over 'til it's over. I don't care how far in front the Aussies are, it's never over. Our business is numbers, son, eyeballs."

This led to a swiftly-booked flight to Sydney, first thing the next morning, and a meeting with Packer at Park Street, where Nicholas was accompanied by co-commentators Mark Taylor and Ian Healy. Beginning with a wider harangue of their commentary, Packer kept the trio in his office for three and a half hours, gradually working his way from the hard messages to quizzing Taylor about the CA Board (Taylor was on the Board from 2004-2018) and Healy about the Australian Cricketers' Association, and then the state of the game in general, batting techniques, golf and tennis. Finally, he left them with a message to remember him by: "Take care of the game, because it won't take care of itself".

The last time Merriman saw Kerry Packer was at the one-off match played between Ricky Ponting's Australians and a World XI at the SCG in October 2005. "I was lucky enough to have Clive Lloyd there, and Tony Greig and Ian Chappell," Merriman says. "Kerry was terribly sick—he hardly ate anything at lunch. In fact, I had to get the car all the way up to where the door was. 'I'll be right son. I'll be all right son', he said. So I sat with them for a couple of minutes, but thought, 'Hang on this isn't where I should be.' There's Clive Lloyd, Tony Greig, Ian Chappell and Kerry. We didn't get a photograph of it but we should have. And then about half an hour later he came up and said, 'Son, seeya 'round', then he just went off, and I never spoke to him again."

With Packer's death that December, a link to cricket's

past was severed, but not forgotten. The Bradman and Packer names were intertwined again in 2013, when a permanent exhibition on WSC was opened at the Bradman Museum, also known as the International Cricket Hall of Fame, in Bowral. On the day that the exhibition opened, Richie Benaud spoke at length about the period between 1977 and 1979, working his way through many of the familiar tales explaining how the war began. Then, with a typical pause and the hint of a grin, he let his audience in on a secret, too. "Many people," Benaud began, "know the story of how World Series Cricket began. But let me tell you how it ended…"

Acknowledgements

lmost six years have passed since this project first entered my mind, when in early 2013 the World Series Cricket exhibition was launched at the Bradman Museum in Bowral. That day the late Richie Benaud not only gave me a tremendous thrill by declaring, upon our introduction to one another, "I read you!", but also provided the germination of the idea by sharing his understanding of how the WSC split ended: through the personal understanding reached by Packer and Bradman. From there, thanks is due to Christian Ryan and Gideon Haigh for encouraging me to pursue the idea, even as others took precedence.

Before becoming a book, the story was first teased out in part as a long-form article for ESPNcricinfo's *The Cricket Monthly* in 2016, and many thanks are due to Osman Samiuddin, Rahul Bhattacharya, Leslie Mathew and Sambit Bal for helping take the story that far and helping to focus it in my mind. It was during this process that I spoke at some length with John Rogers, who was able to provide me with a copy of his 1984 report on cricket's estimated revenue in Australia and otherwise provide lively and thoughtful assistance.

Either side of the initial article and as it began to grow in scope, all interviewees were unceasingly helpful. Particular praise is due to Bob Merriman for the amount of time he gave, while Malcolm Gray's collection of notes from his chairmanship of the ACB and the subsequent 1992 World Cup offered priceless insights. The irrepressible Ronald Cardwell also provided substantial help with finding key documents, as did Gideon Haigh. Cos Cardone and Andrew Jones were both of great assistance in keeping me convinced of the idea's merit.

At Slattery Media Group, Russell Jackson provided plenty of encouragement to get the manuscript started, consistent advice as it progressed, and then deft editing feedback as it evolved into the finished product. Geoff Slattery provided vast experience and his own useful sifting through the manuscript, and Kate Slattery a fitting cover design, bringing together two men who had, of course, never been photographed together.

Constructive reading and feedback was provided by Richard Hinds, George Megalogenis and Izzy Westbury, while friends including Alex McLaren, Cat Rafael, Gaby D'Souza, Adam Collins, Shannon Gill and Kirsten Weiser provided sympathetic ears throughout. Sam

Rogers, a great mate and equally fine housemate, waited patiently while the dining table was buried beneath books, documents and notes. Trish Jha's belief was unfailing, and deeply appreciated.

Sources

BOOKS

Barry, Paul; *The Rise and Rise of Kerry Packer*, Bantam, Sydney, 2007.

Beecher, Eric; *The Cricket Revolution*, Newspress, Melbourne, 1978.

Benaud, Richie (Editor); *Cricket Yearbook 1993*, Hamlyn, Sydney, 1993.

Border, Allan; *Beyond Ten Thousand*, Swan Publishing, Perth, 1993.

Bradman, Don; *Farewell To Cricket*, Hodder and Stoughton, London, 1950.

Chappell, Greg; *Fierce Focus*, Hardie Grant, Melbourne, 2011.

Chenoweth, Neil; *Packer's Lunch*, Allen and Unwin, Sydney, 2006.

Fitzsimons, Peter; *The Rugby War*, Harper Sports, Sydney, 1996.

Geddes, Margaret; *Remembering Bradman*, Penguin/Viking, Melbourne, 2002.

Gibbs, Barry; *My Cricket Journey*, Wakefield Press, Kent Town, 2001.

Greig, Joyce and Greig, Mark; *Tony Greig*, Macmillan, Sydney, 2013.

Haigh, Gideon; *The Cricket War*, Text Publishing, Melbourne, 1993.

Haigh, Gideon; *One Summer, Every Summer*; Text Publishing, Melbourne, 1995.

Haigh, Gideon; *The Summer Game*, Text Publishing, Melbourne, 1997.

Haigh, Gideon and Frith, David; *Inside Story*, News Custom Publishing, Melbourne, 2007.

Halbish, Graham; *Run Out*, Lothian, Melbourne, 2003.

Harte, Chris and Hadfield, Warwick; *Cricket Rebels*; QB Books, Sydney, 1985.

Harte, Chris; *A History of Australian Cricket*, Andre Deutsch, London, 1993.

Kitney, Damon; *The Price Of Fortune*, Harper Collins, Sydney, 2018.

Knox, Malcolm; *Taylor and Beyond*, ABC Books, Sydney, 2000.

Lawson, Geoff; *Henry*, Ironbark Press, Randwick, 1993.

Lee, Alan; *A Pitch in Both Camps*, S. Paul, London, 1979.

Martin, Ray; *Stories Of My Life*, Penguin, Melbourne, 2010.

Martin-Jenkins, Christopher; *Cricket Contest*, Queen Anne Press, London, 1980.

McFarline, Peter; *A Game Divided*; Marlin Books, Melbourne, 1978.

McFarline, Peter; *A Testing Time*, Hutchinson Australia, Melbourne, 1979.

McGregor, Adrian; *Greg Chappell*, Fontana, Sydney, 1986.

Mitchell, Harold; *Living Large*, Melbourne University Press, Melbourne, 2009.

Nicholas, Mark; *A Beautiful Game*; Allen and Unwin, Sydney, 2016.

Ray, Mark; *Border and Beyond*, ABC Books, Sydney, 1995.

Rosenwater, Irving; *Sir Donald Bradman*, Batsford, London, 1978.

Robertson, Austin; *Cricket Outlaws*, Macmillan, Sydney, 2017.

Ryan, Christian; *Golden Boy*, Allen and Unwin, Sydney, 2009.

Speed, Malcolm; *Sticky Wicket*, Harper Sports, Sydney, 2011.

Taylor, Mark; *Taylor Made*, Macmillan, Sydney, 1995.

Taylor, Mark; *Time To Declare*, Macmillan, Sydney, 1999.

Wadhwaney, K. R.; *Gavaskar*, Siddharth Publications, New Delhi, 1996.

Wallace, Christine; *The Private Don*, Allen and Unwin, Sydney, 2004.

Waugh, Steve; *Out of My Comfort Zone*, Penguin, Melbourne, 2005.

Wilde, Simon; *Ian Botham*, Simon and Schuster, London, 2011.

Williams, Charles; *Bradman*, Abacus, London, 2001.

Yallop, Graham; *Lambs To The Slaughter*, Outback Press, Melbourne, 1979.

NEWSPAPERS AND WEBSITES

The Age

The Sydney Morning Herald

The Guardian

The Australian

The Independent

ESPNcricinfo

TELEVISION

Howzat! Kerry Packer's War, (2002), Produced by Endemol Australia

Also from Slattery Media

THE INSTANT CRICKET LIBRARY – BY DAN LIEBKE

In Dan Liebke's debut cricket book, *The Instant Cricket Library*, you'll find excerpts from a number of remarkable cricket books, none of which you've ever read before. There's I, Pad, Shane Watson's infamous manifesto arguing that the LBW Law should be abolished. There's Out of My Ed, in which you'll discover the truth about the real Ed Cowan. There's a Banner-Man comic book, a Mitch Marsh play, and much more. They're all part of the Instant Cricket Library.

Imagine a world after a complete societal collapse. A big collapse, like Australia on a raging Chennai turner. In this dystopian future, all of the world's cricket books have been destroyed. Nothing remains, not even the Steve Waugh autobiographies, which were previously believed to be impervious not just to casual readers, but to all known forms of physical damage. And yet, a hardy group of researchers search desperately for hints of what might have been lost. A title here. A snippet of text there. A tattered cover somewhere else. They gather all the clues they've discovered of the lost world of cricketing literature, and enter them into a hastily constructed supercomputer.

Finally, with a burst of makeshift artificial intelligence, they extrapolate from those fragments and regenerate a complete cricket library in an instant. This instant cricket library is a marvel of resourcefulness, and a glorious tribute to the ingenuity and determination of humanity, even when faced with the most nightmarish and cricketless of futures.

Just because a cricket book never existed doesn't mean it's not worth reading.

Also from Slattery Media

THE NORM SMITH MEDALLISTS
– BY DAN EDDY

The Norm Smith Medal, inaugurated in 1979 and awarded to the best player on AFL Grand Final day, is one of football's highest honours. In this unprecedented survey of the players who strode onto the MCG and dominated the game's most important day, Dan Eddy captures some of footy's most memorable feats in the words of the men whose brilliance turned the contest.

Now, for the first time, football lovers will be taken on a thrilling journey, from each medallist's early days in football, right up until the moment he stood on the presentation dais soaking up the roar of the crowd. Riding every bump, celebrating each goal, and savouring in the unforgettable atmosphere of the day, readers will gain fresh and often surprising insights into classic Grand Final performances of the modern era.

Named for the towering figure of the Melbourne Football Club—a man who played in four Premierships for the Demons and led them to six more in the space of a decade, as the game's most revered and influential coach—the Norm Smith Medal has for five decades honoured the best of the best: the player who performed most brilliantly when the pressure was greatest: on that final Saturday in September.

From Wayne Harmes's unforgettable, team-lifting display in 1979, through Gary Ayres's brave, narrow-eyed brilliance in Hawthorn's swaggering 1980s sides, right up to Dustin Martin's flawless, unprecedented finale to the 2017 season, The Norm Smith Medal is a fascinating account of the game's greatest individual performances.

Also in this series

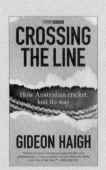

CROSSING THE LINE—HOW AUSTRALIAN CRICKET LOST ITS WAY
BY GIDEON HAIGH

'I'm not proud of what's happened. Y'know, it's not within the spirit of the game.' Steve Smith was not to know it at Cape Town on 24 March 2018, but he was addressing his last press conference as captain of the Australian cricket team. By the next day morning he would be swept from office by a tsunami of public indignation involving even the prime minister.

In a unique admission, Smith confessed to condoning a policy of sandpapering the cricket ball in a Test against South Africa. He, the instigator David Warner and their agent Cameron Bancroft returned home to disgrace and to lengthy bans. The crisis plunged Australian cricket into a bout of unprecedented soul searching, with Cricket Australia yielding to demands for reviews of the cricket team and of itself to restore confidence in their 'culture'.

In *Crossing the Line—How Australian cricket lost its way,* Gideon Haigh conducts his own cultural review – 'less official and far cheaper but genuinely independent'. Studying the cricket team across a decade of radical change, he finds an accident waiting to happen, and a system struggling to cope with self-created challenges, on the field and in the boardroom. And he wonders: is there even any longer a spirit of the game to be within?

PRAISE FOR *CROSSING THE LINE:*

"A remarkable feat of pulling focus in a short time. It is full of grainy detail without blurring the big picture. As ever in Haigh's writing, the prose is deft and distinctive, worth reading in its own right, but above all made to serve the project of forensic fact-gathering and logical storytelling."
– GREG BAUM, *THE AGE*

"A devastating account of the effects of the professionalization of cricket, providing context and critical understanding to the crisis of Cape Town."
– MIKE ATHERTON

"Haigh delivers knowledge and insight in cogent, digestible form, condensing his intimate understanding of complex, long-term processes and intangible forces into a neat package that leaves the reader with a fresh understanding."
- WISDEN